entertain

Happy Birthday all my love.

entertain
ed baines

with photographs by Gus Filgate

KYLE BOOKS

Edited by **Lewis Esson**

Design by **Mark Latter at Vivid Design**

Photography by **Gus Filgate assisted by Will Heap**

Food preparation **Ed Baines and Linda Tubby**

Recipe testing **Ed Baines and Jacqueline Clarke**

Styling by **Helen Trent**

Production by **Lorraine Baird and Sha Huxtable**

All recipes serve 4 unless otherwise stated.

This edition published in 2004 by Kyle Books,
an imprint of Kyle Cathie Limited.
general.enquiries@kyle-cathie.com
www.kylecathie.com

Distributed by National Book Network
4501 Forbes Blvd., Suite 200
Lanham, MD 20706
Phone: (301) 459 3366
Fax: (301) 429 5746

10 9 8 7 6 5 4 3 2 1

ISBN 1 904920 05 5

The Library of Congress Cataloguing-in-Publication Data
is available on file.

Colour separations by Scanhouse
Printed in Singapore by Tien Wah Press Pte Ltd

contents

acknowledgements

My thanks for the enormous support and help from a great team
that I work with, and Minnie. I would also like to say a big 'thank
you' to my business partner Jamie for being so very much a
partner in the last five years. Also to my chef Alan, who has been
my right-hand man for the past six years and, more recently,
Paul, who does a sterling job at the helm of Soho; and for the
dedication from Christian. Thanks also to Daniel, as our company
really benefits from his wonderful ability to throw amazing bashes
on a regular basis. He is one of the few men I know who can
successfully host a big party every night of the week, every week
of the year. Finally, a special thank-you to my mum, my two
brothers and my son, whom I love deeply. Each in their own ways
has always helped me jump hurdles. Even Louis, at the grand old
age of five, insists he will come to work with Dad and help, and
often compliments me on being a 'good cooker'.

introduction

Why do I cook? I've always had an enormous interest in food, ever since I can remember, although I had no idea that it would eventually lead to me becoming a professional chef. As a child, I was forever asking my Mum what was coming up next. We were enormously fortunate in having an extremely varied diet and my Mum only ever gave us fresh foods.

As kids, the three Baines brothers went on local shopping trips and there was a real understanding of the produce being sold by each specialized proprietor, be it a deli or a vegetable store. Unfortunately, the craft of shop-keeping is fast disappearing and more emphasis has been placed on the consumer to be able to recognize quality.

My first job in catering arose from an infatuation with the pâtisserie on Chiswick High Road in London. I decided rather than stare at the cakes I

would ask for a job, and got one as a junior assistant the following day. After working there for a year, my chef believed I had the ability to move and shake in the business and suggested I went up to the Dorchester Hotel for a thorough training. Since my apprenticeship at the Dorch, I've had a wonderful career to date, often being lucky enough to find myself in the right place at the right time.

Throughout my early years of catering I had one dream and that was to open a restaurant. My inspiration was the famous

Edward Hopper painting of a café at night called
Nighthawks. I found a similar-looking cafe in
Melbourne, which had the appearance and ambience of
a diner, but served the most wonderful, healthy food.
This was the model for our first restaurant Randall &
Aubin, Brewer Street. Although it was even harder to
achieve than I could ever have imagined, after many
years of unceasing work, it is now successful.

I have since opened two more restaurants, but
remain hands-on in all aspects of the business. The
most wonderful thing, apart from the diversity of people
you meet, is creating your own business and, touch
wood, the operation becoming successful. However
demanding it may be, feeding 3,000 plus people a week
to a high standard is a uniquely rewarding task.

More recently, out of the blue, something happened
that I had never really considered. I was asked if I was interested in
presenting a television show. I gave it my all, although in all honesty I was
quite terrified at first, and this new career now seems to be developing in the
right direction – with the fourth series under my belt, another currently
running on the Carlton Food Network, and various guest appearances on an
assortment of shows.

I know an awful lot of chefs – myself included before the birth of my first
son – who never cook or eat in their own homes. Over the last five years, as a
father, I can tell you've I've spent many hours cooking at home with my son,
my brother Jon and friends with their kids. It has surprised me how easily I
adapted to becoming Mr Mum and, with my new-found confidence, I even
recently declared that I would like to have five children to feed and raise.

What I would really love is for you to use this book and enjoy it with your
families. Nearly every recipe, bar those in the Dining chapter (which contains a

few major challenges), was written in and for the domestic kitchen rather than the professional environment. And, quite honestly, there is no comparison. At work, the first rule of menu writing is to do what cannot be done at home. The second is make as much mess as you like, 'cos there's always someone around to clean up. In our home lives today, however, we all have limited time and space to cook. I really do feel all these recipes are achievable even for a beginner; just give yourself a little bit of time, and avoid getting frustrated. Cooking is a little like model-making, the moment you get upset it will go wrong.

One thing you may notice is that certain chapters don't have desserts. The reason for this is that a simple lunch will not really be particularly simple if you make a tiramisu for it, and I think it would be rather patronizing of me to include a very obvious recipe of, say, strawberries and cream or cheese and fruit. Of course, you must feel free to mix and match and get creative throughout the chapters.

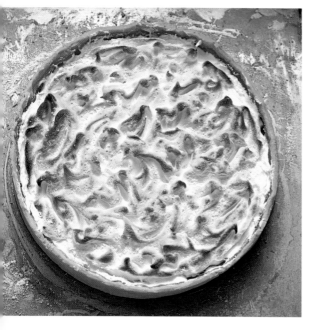

Always try to create a balanced meal, with the right mix of protein, carbohydrate and fiber: for example roast ham with a lentil salad and braised broccoli. It's been noticed that I use a lot of olive oil in my recipes, but I have spent a lot of time training in Italy and the South of France, and people there are far healthier. Oil lubricates your digestive system and olive oil, in particular, has a wide range of beneficial effects, from warding off heart disease and cancer to promoting longevity. Indeed, among the healthiest people in the world are the Cretans, who consume more olive oil per head than anywhere else in Europe. I even argued once, many years ago, that drinking it neat wasn't a problem.

You'll also notice that among my favorite aromatic flavoring ingredients is the grated rind of various citrus

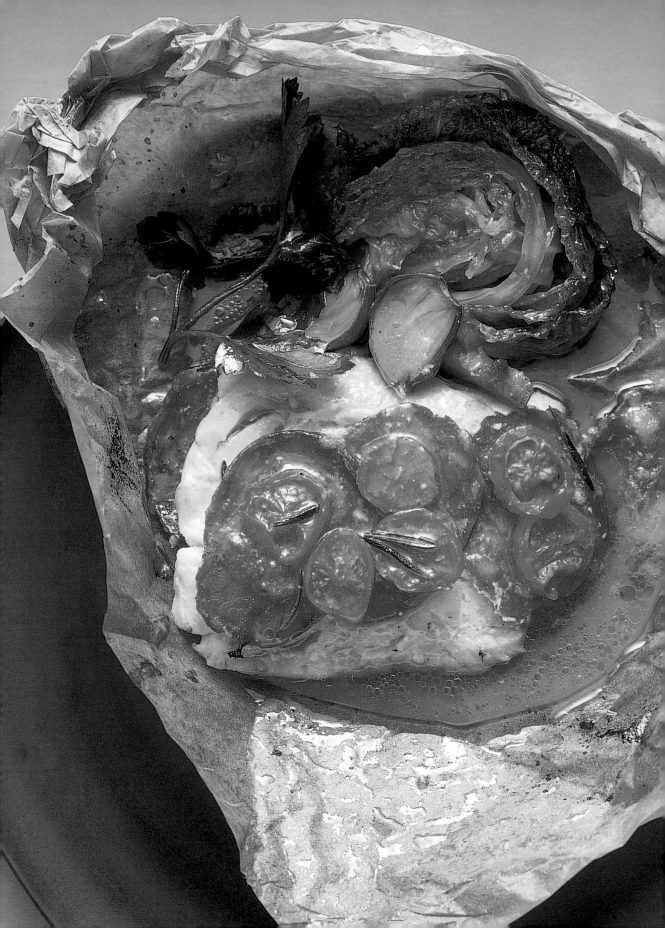

fruits, like lemons, limes, and oranges. I just adore them for the freshness and zing they impart. However, you do have to remember that most citrus fruit nowadays is coated with a layer of wax impregnated with various chemicals to help prolong shelf-life. So, if you are going to be adding citrus rind to your food, try to find organic uncoated fruit or scrub them well in hot soapy water and rinse thoroughly before use.

It is so important to use good natural ingredients; the best you can afford. Looks can be deceiving; for example the perfect looking zucchini is often watery and tasteless, whereas a home-grown, rough-and-ready one, left to nature, will usually ping with flavor. I realized this while working in Italy, where we produced all our own fruit and vegetables, and had the direct link from nature to my stove. It was magical. We pressed our own oils and collected our own fresh figs straight off the tree.

We can't always enjoy such bounty on our doorsteps, but I hope some of the recipes in this book will help you experience just a little of the enjoyment I have had from food through the years.

Brunch is probably among my favorite meals, built around the sort of relaxed straightforward dishes you can just rock out of bed after a heavy night out and make almost without thinking, but full of flavor to perk up the palate and substantial enough to soak up your hangover.

Back in my days at Daphne's, Sunday brunches were among the busiest sessions of the week and, although they were undoubtedly a lovely experience for the clientele, I'd usually have to struggle through, due to my Saturday nights out, hauling my way through cracking hundreds of eggs, with the occasional perk-up of a bloody Mary.

The opportunities I've had to eat brunch on a Sunday myself have often extended themselves all the way to lunch and once even to dinner, a practice which comes highly recommended.

brunches

potato rösti
with bacon & eggs

Potato rösti is a speciality of Switzerland and to make it properly you have to take on the swish Swiss way of doing things. Once mastered, though, it's a great accompaniment to fish, meat, and vegetarian dishes. In Switzerland, rösti is often used as a base for something similar to pizza, where toppings can be added. For this brunch recipe we're using bacon and eggs.

First peel the potatoes and then shred them into a colander. Squeeze the shredded potato to remove as much water as possible (use your hands to do this rather than a dish towel) – the drier the potatoes the better. Add a pinch of nutmeg with some salt and pepper to the dry shredded potato and mix well.

Heat 2 tablespoons of olive oil and 1 tablespoon of butter gently in a 6 inch skillet. Add a quarter of the potato to the pan over a medium heat. Mold the potato to fill the base of the pan by pushing it down firmly with a wooden spatula or spoon. Cook over medium heat for 4–5 minutes until golden and lightly crisp on the underside then, using your spatula, turn the rösti over, press it down again and cook for a further 4–5 minutes. Remove from the pan and allow to rest on a cooling rack or paper towels. Repeat to make 3 more.

Preheat a hot broiler. Broil the bacon until just nicely crisp at the edges. At the same time fry the eggs gently in a little oil until the whites are set but the yolks are still runny. Arrange the bacon on top of the röstis and top with the eggs. Serve.

2 large potatoes

a pinch of freshly grated nutmeg

salt and pepper

8 tablespoons olive oil (traditionally lard or pork fat is used)

2 ounces (½ stick) unsalted butter

8 slices of bacon

8 eggs

eggs benedict

This is one of my most popular brunch dishes and, although very simple, the quality of the ham, poached egg and hollandaise are all vital for the success of this recipe.

First make the hollandaise sauce: put all the ingredients except the butter, eggs, salt and cayenne in a saucepan, bring to a boil and reduce by half. Pull from the heat and allow to cool.

Using a bain-marie (or a bowl set over a saucepan of heated water), first clarify your butter by placing it in a large heatproof bowl set in the bain-marie and allowing it to melt gently until it separates, the whey falling to the bottom. Remove the bowl from the heat, carefully ladle the clear butter into a heatproof container and place to one side. Discard the whey and wash the mixing bowl, then dry thoroughly.

Now place the egg yolks and 2 tablespoons of the cooled infusion in the mixing bowl and, ensuring the water in the saucepan is over medium heat, place the bowl in the bain-marie or over the saucepan and whisk continuously until the yolks start to become firm. Remove the bowl from the heat and place on a flat surface, wrapping a dish towel around the bowl to stop it slipping.

Start to whisk the egg yolks vigorously and, while continuing to whisk, slowly start to add the clarified butter. Keep slowly pouring in the butter until it is all blended, then continue to whisk while adding one more dessertspoon of the infusion until fully blended. Finally add a pinch of salt and some cayenne pepper.

Cut the English muffins in half and lightly toast the halves on both sides. Cover the 8 muffin halves with the ham. Preheat a hot broiler.

Fill a large saucepan (16 inch is best) with water to a depth of about 4 inches. Stir in the vinegar and a good pinch of salt. Bring the water to a boil, then turn the heat down to the lowest possible. Crack each of the eggs into a small ramekin. Using a whisk, create a whirlpool in the water, then carefully put each egg into the hot water by placing the rim of the ramekin into the moving edge of the water and gently tipping in the egg. Repeat with the remaining eggs as quickly as possible and allow each to cook for 1–1½ minutes. Using a slotted spoon, remove the eggs as they are cooked and gently place on a plate.

Flash the English muffins under the broiler for 1 minute. Place an egg on top of each of the hammed muffin halves. Spoon hollandaise over them and place under the broiler again until the sauce is golden brown. Serve with a twist of black pepper.

For a really special occasion, make Eggs Benedict Royale in exactly the same way, but replacing the ham with smoked salmon and topping the muffin halves with caviar just before serving.

4 English muffins

8 ounces sliced honey roast ham

2 tablespoons vinegar (any kind that you have to hand)

8 large eggs

for the hollandaise sauce

½ wine glass of white wine vinegar

½ wine glass of white wine

5 black peppercorns

1 garlic clove

2–3 parsley stalks

juice of 1 lemon

6 ounces butter (1½ sticks)

4 egg yolks

a pinch of salt

cayenne pepper

perfect scrambled eggs
with smoked salmon & truffle oil

First things first…although I am sure we can all make scrambled eggs,
as a chef I am often asked how to 'do them like you do'.

Crack the eggs into a bowl and start to whisk. Add 2½ ounces (5 tablespoons)
melted butter and the milk, and continue whisking until light and fluffy. Season
with salt.

   Add the remaining butter to a large saucepan and gently melt it on a very low
heat. Remove the pan from heat.

   While it melts, toast the bread on both sides and place in the bottom of the
broiler under the broiler tray to keep it warm but not to cook it. It is very important
to make the toast first as once the eggs are cooked you need to serve them
immediately and you don't want to be flapping around making toast.

   Add the egg mixture to the pan, turn the heat to moderate-to-hot and stir
constantly with a spatula once the mixture starts to form lumps at the edges.
Continue to stir, drawing the edges in until cooked but still slightly liquid in the
center. Pull the pan from heat, add the smoked salmon, and stir in well.

   Put the toast on plates and spoon the scrambled eggs and salmon over the
toast. Due to the heat of the pan, the final part of this cooking process takes place
off the stove. Finally drizzle with truffle oil for that gourmet finish. In my experience,
truffle oil is an acquired taste – once acquired, extend your shopping budget.

6 large very fresh eggs (at
room temperature if
possible)

4 ounces (1 stick) unsalted
butter

¼ pint (⅔ cup) milk

salt and pepper

4 slices of crusty bread

4 ounces chopped
smoked salmon

a few drops of truffle oil,
to serve (optional)

white risotto
with eggs & parmesan

Melt half the butter in a large saucepan with the olive oil. Slice the leeks lengthwise, then wash them thoroughly and chop finely. Add the onion, garlic, celery, and leeks to the melted butter and oil. Allow the vegetables to sweat gently over a low heat for 10 minutes, stirring occasionally.

While the vegetables are cooking, in a separate saucepan gently heat the vegetable broth and milk. Add the rice to the vegetables and increase the heat to moderate-to-high. Stir for 2 minutes and add the white wine, then slowly add the hot stock and milk, bit by bit, to the rice over 20 minutes, stirring occasionally, until it is cooked but still firm to the bite. Pull the saucepan from the heat and add two-thirds of the Parmesan and the remaining butter, stirring vigorously. Preheat the broiler to full whack.

Spoon the risotto out on to 4 heatproof serving plates and create a well in the center of each portion. Crack an egg into each well and dust with the remaining Parmesan and black pepper. Place under the broiler until the egg is cooked to soft yolk, about 3 minutes. Serve with a salad of mixed green leaves tossed in Balsamic Dressing.

The method opposite for poaching fish, i.e. bringing it to a boil and then allowing it to cool back down to room temperature in the liquid, will always ensure perfect poaching! Use this same method when poaching salmon, for instance.

This white risotto with eggs and Parmesan is an Austro-Hungarian adaptation of the classic Italian recipe.

4 ounces (1 stick) unsalted butter
2 tablespoons olive oil
2 leeks
1 large onion, finely chopped
2 garlic cloves, finely chopped
4 celery stalks, finely chopped
2 pints (5 cups) vegetable broth
1 pint (2½ cups) milk
10½ ounces (2⅔ cups) Arborio rice
2 glasses of white wine
2 ounces (1 cup) Parmesan cheese
4 large eggs
salad of green leaves tossed in Balsamic Dressing (page 253), to serve

smoked haddock rarebit

Welsh rarebit is the much loved inspiration for this dish. When buying your smoked haddock, don't be deceived into going for the bright yellow variety, as it is not traditional and is, in fact, dyed and nasty. The haddock should be cooked in milk, which then becomes a wonderful ingredient for mixing with vegetable broth to add to risottos or pasta dishes.

½ pint (1¼ cups) milk

1 bay leaf

4 black peppercorns

a bunch of parsley

1 pound haddock fillets

2 ounces (½ stick) unsalted butter

2 ounces (½ cup) all-purpose flour

2 ounces (¾ cup) mature Cheddar cheese, shredded

1 teaspoon English mustard

2 egg yolks

1 tablespoon Worcestershire sauce

juice of ½ lemon

pepper

4 nice chunky slices of bread

4 tomatoes, quartered, seeded and chopped

Pour the milk into a large saucepan, add the bay leaf, peppercorns, parsley stalks, and haddock fillets (skin side up) and bring to a boil over a medium heat. Remove from the heat, cover, and allow to cool. Once cooled, remove the haddock from the liquid, put it on a plate, and place to one side.

In a separate saucepan, gently melt the butter with the flour, stirring to make a paste. Strain the poaching milk into the butter-and-flour paste. Do this slowly, bit by bit, to ensure a smooth consistency, stirring continuously, until all the milk has been added. Cook for 5 minutes, then remove from the heat. Add the shredded cheese and mustard. Remove the skin from the haddock and flake the flesh into the sauce. Add the egg yolks, Worcestershire sauce, lemon juice, finely chopped parsley, and pepper. No need to add salt as there is already enough in the haddock. Pour the mixture into a bowl, cover, and place in refridgerator.

Preheat a hot broiler and toast the bread under it on full heat until lightly browned on one side only. Remove and spread the finely chopped tomatoes over the untoasted side. Now add a good dollop of the rarebit mixture to each slice of tomato bread and broil until golden brown. (After writing this recipe, we're all starving and are now going to tuck into some haddock rarebit ourselves.)

If you like, you could do a Tuscan variation of this pasta recipe using cannellini beans and shredded Savoy cabbage.

linguine
with fresh pesto & potato

I was first shown this dish by a wonderful Italian chef, Massimo, who worked with me at Daphne's. He was a rarity among Italian chefs in London as he was from the north, Milan to be exact, and although northerners do tend to be better chefs, they don't usually gravitate over here as life at home is just too good. In true Italian style, he was taught this simple and fantastic recipe by his mother.

First make the pesto: put 4 tablespoons of olive oil in a 10 inch skillet and place over moderate heat. Add the pine nuts and fry gently for 2 minutes, moving them constantly. Remove from the heat and allow the pine nuts to continue cooking gently off the heat.

Roughly chop the basil, stalks and all, and put in a mixing bowl. Add all the Parmesan, the lemon juice, and the remaining olive oil, then pour in the pine nuts with their oil. Using the end of a rolling pin or something similar, grind the mixture to a paste. You have made Pesto Genovese.

Peel the potatoes and slice them into thin disks, then cut the disks into thin slices. Turn the slices and cut them into cubes. Place all the potato cubes in a bowl half-filled with water to help wash away the starch.

Heat the olive oil in a skillet and add the drained and dried potato cubes. Stir continuously until golden brown and crispy. Add the finely chopped garlic to the potatoes, then pour the potatoes into a strainer placed over a bowl to catch any juices.

Bring a large saucepan of salted water to a boil. Add the linguine and cook for 8 minutes, stirring occasionally. While the pasta cooks, add the potatoes and garlic to the pesto.

Drain the cooked pasta and then return to the saucepan. Add the pesto and potato mixture and stir gently. Add the mascarpone with the vegetable broth and mix together well over a gentle heat. Season.

2 large potatoes

4 tablespoons olive oil

2 garlic cloves, finely chopped

14 ounces (5⅓ cups) of dried linguine

salt and pepper

1 tablespoon mascarpone cheese

¼ pint (⅝ cup) vegetable broth

for the pesto

6½ fluid ounces (¾ cup) olive oil

9 ounces (2½ cups) pine nuts

2 bunches of basil

5 ounces Parmesan cheese, finely shredded

juice of 1 lemon

homemade blinis
with smoked salmon & crème fraîche

Although blinis are now pretty readily available in supermarkets, they are quite simple to make at home – and a whole lot better. For this recipe, they are the only thing that require cooking, so give them a go. There are many different recipes for blinis, but this one is a firm favorite at the restaurant in Soho, London.

First make the blinis: mix the yeast with the water and leave for 5 minutes until frothy. Put the yeast mixture, milk, flour, egg yolks, salt, sugar, and melted butter in a blender and whiz for 40 seconds. Scrape the mixture down the sides and whiz again for a few seconds. Pour the batter into a large bowl and cover loosely. Leave to rise in a warm place for 1½–2 hours. (Don't leave it any longer, or the blinis will taste over-fermented.)

Beat the egg whites until stiff and fold into the risen batter. Heat a griddle or heavy saucepan, brush with butter and drop teaspoonfuls of the batter on it. When bubbles start to appear on the surface, turn the blinis over and cook for a few minutes longer. They should be lightly browned on both sides. Keep the blinis warm while making the rest.

Now lay the smoked salmon out on a large plate and place to one side (it always tastes better at room temperature). Finely chop the chives and place them in a bowl with a pinch of salt and the olive oil. Add the crème fraîche and mix thoroughly. Using a teaspoon, place a small amount of crème fraîche mixture on each blini, then place a piece of salmon on top. Finally, using the handle of the teaspoon, place a small amount of roe or caviar on top of the crème fraîche. Serve with lemon wedges and black pepper.

8 ounces sliced smoked salmon

a bunch of chives

salt and pepper

1 tablespoon olive oil

8 fluid ounces (1 cup) crème fraîche

¾ ounce lumpfish roe, Avruga (Spanish herring roe) or, if budget permits, Russian or Iranian caviar

1 lemon, cut into wedges, to serve

for the blinis

¾ ounce dried yeast

3¾ fluid ounces (½ cup) warm water

8 fluid ounces (1 cup) milk

8 ounces (2 cups) all-purpose flour

3 eggs, separated

½ teaspoon salt

a pinch of sugar

2¾ ounces (5 tablespoons) melted butter, plus more for greasing

crispy cod fingers
with tomato, zucchini, & olive compote

Homemade fish fingers always go down a treat so, whether cooking for
adults or kids, this one is always a winner. If you don't have the time, you
could just buy pre-made cod fingers and spend your time making the compote.
You can also adapt the recipe for any fresh fish, like haddock or flounder.

First make the compote: bring to a boil 3 pints of water. Using a sharp knife, score a
cross in the tops of the tomatoes, then put them into the boiling water for 10
seconds. Drain and immediately place in iced water. Now peel the skins from the
tomatoes and cut into quarters, then cut the quarters in half again to form rough
cubes. Cut the zucchini in half lengthwise, then cut these halves lengthwise again
and across to form cubes.

Pour the olive oil into a 14 inch saucepan or cooking pot. Add the onions and
garlic and cook over moderate-to-high heat, stirring occasionally. When they have
softened, add the zucchini, turn the heat up to high and seal the zucchini for 3
minutes. Reduce the heat to low-to-moderate and add the tomatoes, olives,
anchovies, vinegar, sugar, whole basil leaves, lime juice, a pinch of salt, and a twist
of pepper. Stir all the ingredients together and reduce the heat to the lowest possible.
Leave to cook gently on the back of the stove while you prepare the fish fingers.

Make the fish fingers: cut the cod fillets across in quarters, turn each quarter
around and cut them lengthwise to form fingers. You'll get 3–5 fingers per quarter,
depending on the shape of the fillet.

Crack both eggs into a mixing bowl and whisk in the milk. Put the flour in a
separate bowl and the breadcrumbs in another. Add the lime rind to the
breadcrumbs, together with the dried oregano and a good pinch of salt. Put the cod
fingers in the flour and cover gently but thoroughly, then individually dip them into
the egg mixture. Finally, roll each finger through the breadcrumbs, patting the
breadcrumbs firmly on to the fish to form a coat. Place carefully on a baking sheet.

At this point give your compote a gentle stir. Heat the oil in a large skillet for a
couple of minutes over a moderate heat. Put your fish fingers into the pan, 6 at a
time, cooking until golden-brown on all sides. Put the cooked fish fingers on paper
towel to soak up any excess oil and repeat until all fingers are cooked. Remove the
compote from heat and stir again. Put a large spoonful in the center of each plate
and arrange the fish fingers slightly overlapping on the side of the compote.

2 pounds skinned cod
fillets, any pin bones
removed

2 eggs

3½ fluid ounces (⅓ cup) milk

8 ounces (2 cups)
all-purpose flour

4 ounces Japanese
breadcrumbs

finely shredded rind of 2
limes

1 teaspoon dried oregano

a pinch of salt

4 tablespoons vegetable oil

**for the tomato, zucchini,
& olive compote**

8 tomatoes

iced water

1 pound zucchini

¼ pint (⅔ cup) olive oil

1 red onion, roughly chopped

2 garlic cloves, chopped

2 ounces mixed pitted
olives, roughly chopped

2 anchovy fillets, chopped

1 tablespoon white wine
vinegar

1 level tablespoon
granulated sugar

a bunch of basil

juice of 2 limes

salt and pepper

Whenever you are cooking liver, it is best to do it quickly over a very high heat, otherwise it will toughen and dry out – never overcook it.

When buying calves' liver, look for pieces that are a healthy-looking uniform pale pink color, with no discolored patches, and a nice fresh clean smell. Get the butcher to remove any covering membrane for you.

tuscan liver
with caramelized balsamic & watercress mash

I learnt this method for cooking liver from the then manager of Daphne's, Araldo Panacalli, whose cooking, like his personality, made him one in a million.

8 slices of calves' liver, each about 2 ounces and ¼ inch thick

1 onion, finely chopped

2 garlic cloves, finely chopped

6 tablespoons olive oil

6 tablespoons balsamic vinegar

a bunch of flat-leaf parsley, chopped

¼ pint (⅔ cup) fresh beef broth

2 ounces (½ stick) butter

for the watercress mash

4 potatoes

salt and pepper

¼ pint (⅔ cup) milk

4 tablespoons olive oil

a pinch of freshly shredded nutmeg

a bunch of watercress, roughly chopped

First make the mash: peel the potatoes and quarter them, then add to at least 3½ pints of boiling salted water. Cook until soft, drain and add back to the pan to dry over a gentle heat. Start to mash the potatoes, while slowly adding the milk, olive oil, and nutmeg. Once you have a nice purée, pull the pan to one side, and add the watercress. Stir well and leave to rest.

Cut the slices of liver into fine strips. Chop the onion and garlic as fine as you possibly can. Ensure all these ingredients are to hand and prepared before you start cooking.

Heat the olive oil in a large skillet, add the onions and garlic and cook vigorously for 2 minutes. When the pan is extremely hot, add the liver and stir until colored on both sides to a light brown. Add the balsamic vinegar and stir it in quickly, allowing it to caramelize around the strips of liver. Making sure the pan is still intensely hot, stir in the chopped parsley and quickly add the beef broth, which will come to a boil immediately. Add the butter, stir quickly and remove from the heat.

Plate up the mash with the liver on top, spoon over the remaining pan juices, and serve immediately.

In this chapter I have collected together some recipes that are fairly simple and quick to put together – nothing taking more than about half an hour to prepare – so you can make something really nice for lunch and still have time to relax.

Although convenience food is playing a greater role in our day-to-day eating, especially around lunchtime, it is still important to cook and eat fresh food, especially when there are children involved.

A little bit of forward planning makes things an awful lot easier; for example, cook something up on a Tuesday night for Wednesday lunch. I haven't included desserts in this chapter, as most desserts are neither simple nor quick, except things like fruit salad or ice-cream, which are fairly obvious and don't need me to tell you how to make them. There are ample dessert recipes throughout this book, so you can always raid one from another chapter.

lunches

This is a very good dish to make in bulk as it freezes very well. For this reason I've doubled the quantities. It is a favorite at Randall & Aubin, and seconds are regularly ordered.

tomato & lentil soup
with corn bread & crème fraîche

Put the olive oil in a large saucepan, add the lentils, carrots, celery, garlic, and onion. Cook over a very low heat, stirring occasionally, for 10 minutes. Add the sugar and basil, and cook for a further 2 minutes, then add the tomatoes with their liquid and reduce by two-thirds. Pour in the vegetable broth, season with salt and pepper, and bring to a boil. Reduce the heat and simmer for 40–60 minutes. Finish with a pinch of chopped parsley.

To make the corn bread: preheat the oven to 375°F and grease an 8 inch cake pan with butter. In a large bowl, mix together the flour, salt, baking powder, sugar, and cornmeal. Add the eggs, milk, and tablespoon of melted butter, and mix together well to make a smooth mixture. Pour the mixture into the cake pan and bake in the oven for 25 minutes, until the corn bread is golden and springy but firm to the touch. If you can time it right, serve it still warm with the soup and covered in crème fraîche.

4 tablespoons olive oil

4 ounces (½ cup) Puy lentils

4 carrots, finely chopped

½ head of celery, finely chopped

4 garlic cloves, finely chopped

1 Spanish onion, finely chopped

2 teaspoons sugar

a bunch of basil, finely chopped

4 x 14 ounce cans of tomatoes

2 pints (5 cups) vegetable broth

salt and pepper

a small bunch of flat-leaf parsley, finely chopped

9 fluid ounces (1 cup) crème fraîche, to serve

for the corn bread (makes 1 loaf)

1 tablespoon melted butter, plus more for greasing

5 ounces (1¼ cups) all-purpose flour

¼ teaspoon salt

4 teaspoons baking powder

1¾ ounces (¼ cup) superfine sugar

5 ounces (1 cup) yellow cornmeal

2 medium eggs

8 fluid ounces (1 cup) milk

Serves 8

chickpea & mint soup
with haloumi, hummus, and croutons

This is a great soup, whether hot or cold, and really can be eaten as a one-course meal.

Put the olive oil in a large saucepan (big enough take up to 3–4 pints of liquid). Chop the garlic, onion, and celery finely, reserving one whole clove of garlic for the croutons, and add to the pan. Put the pan over a medium heat and cook for 4–5 minutes, then add the chickpeas to the pan and cook for a further 10 minutes. Now add the finely chopped mint, stirring well, and then pour over the vegetable broth and the tahini. Bring to a boil, reduce the heat to low and simmer for at least 30 minutes.

To make the croutons: preheat a medium broiler. Slice the baguette at an angle into long thin slices. Lay the slices out on an oven tray and brush all over with olive oil. Gently broil both sides until golden brown. Rub each piece of toasted baguette with the garlic clove. Thinly slice the cheese and place on top. Put under the broiler for 1 minute, remove and place to one side.

Once the soup is cooked, mash the solids gently with a potato masher. Place back on the heat and cook for a further 5 minutes. Serve with the croutons, a dollop of hummus, and a twist of pepper. You probably won't need to add salt because of the salt content of the vegetable broth.

4 tablespoons olive oil

1 head of garlic

1 small onion

4 celery stalks

1 14 ounce can of chickpeas, drained

a bunch of mint, finely chopped

2 pints (5 cups) vegetable broth

1 tablespoon tahini

1 small pot of hummus, to serve

pepper

for the croutons

1 baguette

4 tablespoons olive oil

4 ounces of haloumi cheese

Adding lemon juice to the water when cooking artichokes prevents them discoloring.

sausages en papillote
with onion, garlic, & lemon rind, broiled artichokes, & mustard beans

Preheat the oven to 350°F. Using a bread knife in a clockwise direction, trim off the outside leaves of the artichokes. Bring to a boil a large saucepan of salted water acidulated with the juice of ½ lemon and boil the artichokes for 30 minutes.

While they boil, rip off a 20 inch sheet of aluminum foil, place it on a work surface and drizzle with olive oil. Place 2 sausages on the foil, sprinkle with a quarter of the grated lemon rind and a quarter each of the sliced onion, garlic, and paprika. Fold the foil over gently, sealing the edges to create a loose parcel. Repeat with the remaining sausages to make 4 parcels in all. Place your parcels in the oven and cook for 20 minutes.

Preheat a hot broiler. Drain the artichokes and, using a small knife, cut them into quarters, removing any leathery leaves and the hairs from the chokes. Place the artichoke quarters on a lightly oiled baking sheet, squeeze lemon juice over them and lightly broil for 5 minutes.

Bring another saucepan of salted water to a boil and top and tail the beans. Blanch them for 4 minutes, then drain and tip into a large bowl. Add the artichokes and mix well. Whisk all the dressing ingredients together, then season to taste. Pour the dressing over the vegetables and toss to coat them evenly.

Serve the sausages with the dressed beans and artichokes.

4 globe artichokes

salt and pepper

finely shredded rind of 1 lemon and juice of ½ lemon

2 tablespoons olive oil

8 best-quality butcher's fresh sausages

1 Spanish onion, sliced

4 garlic cloves, sliced

4 pinches of paprika

10 ounces fine green beans

for the dressing

2 teaspoons Dijon mustard

1 tablespoon white wine vinegar

1 egg yolk

¼ pint (⅔ cup) olive oil

pizza eduardo

First make the dough: pour the flour into a large mixing bowl, make a well in the middle and add all the other ingredients. Mix very well to a firm paste for at least 5 minutes, kneading and getting air into the dough. Place the dough in the refridgerator while you prepare the other ingredients.

Make the base sauce: put the garlic in a bowl with the tomatoes, oregano, olive oil, and a pinch of salt. Mix well and place to one side.

Prepare the toppings of your choice in advance (the ones listed here are my favorites, hence the pizza's name), so you're ready to work very quickly once the dough is rolled out. Turn the oven on to full heat.

Remove the dough from the refridgerator and dust your work surface with flour. Take a piece of dough the size of a baseball (How big is a baseball? Smaller than a tennis ball and bigger than a golf ball), roll it out into a circle about ¾ inch thick and slowly, using your hands, turn the circle to stretch it to a round with a diameter of about 12 inches and repeat (this quantity of dough will make 6–8 pizza bases, so you can make more for second helpings.)

Preheat the oven to 425°F. Place the pizza bases on a baking sheet, if any holes appear during transfer just patch them up with a little bit of dough trimmings. Spoon on the tomato sauce, smearing it all over each base, and now add your toppings. Season with the thyme, lemon rind, and salt and pepper, then cook in the hot oven for 4–5 minutes until the dough is nicely colored and the cheese has melted.

Serve with a handful of arugula and Parmesan shavings sprinkled over the top of each pizza.

If you can lay your hands on one, a nice (well-scrubbed, of course) flat stone (like a paving stone) that will fit in your oven, used instead of a baking sheet, makes the most superb pizzas.

You can make the pizza bases well ahead and freeze them. When you put the pizza dough to rest in the fridge, first give it a light spray or brush it with a very little water and this will help prevent any hard crust forming as the dough rises slightly.

for the dough

2 pounds 2 ounces 00 (doppio zero) flour

7 fluid ounces (¾ cup) milk

¾ ounce fresh yeast

½ pint (1¼ cups) mineral water

a good pinch of salt

1 tablespoon olive oil

for the base sauce

1 garlic clove, chopped

1 14 ounce can of plum tomatoes, drained and finely chopped

a pinch of dried oregano

1 tablespoon extra-virgin olive oil

salt and pepper

suggested toppings

6 artichoke hearts (see page 36), sliced

2 ounces Gorgonzola cheese, crumbled

4 ounces pancetta, cut into lardon strips

7 ounces (2 cups) black pitted olives, halved

a bunch of thyme, stalked and finely chopped

finely shredded rind of 1 lemon

to serve

about 4 ounces wild arugula

4 ounces Parmesan cheese in a piece

Do not rush sealing the meat as you want to get it nice and brown, to help develop a good strong flavor.

Cooking the parsley briefly in the mash gives it a much nicer taste and boiling the garlic first eliminates the sharp flavor.

honey-glazed gammon,
carrot, & potato mash

Place a large flameproof casserole dish on a low heat and gently melt the butter with the olive oil. Add the gammon and seal until golden on both sides, about 10 minutes. Remove the gammon and place to one side.

Now add the garlic, onions, and apple to the casserole and cook until the onion is translucent. Add the flour and cook for 1 minute. Add the cider, bring to boil and reduce by half. Then add the Piccalilli, honey, sage leaves, and mustard, and cook for 5 minutes. Season.

Now put the gammon steaks back into the casserole, squeeze in the lemon juice and pour in the broth. Add another good pinch of salt and pepper, cover and simmer for a further 20–30 minutes.

While the gammon simmers, make the mash: half-fill a saucepan with water (about 3½ pints), add salt, cover and bring to a boil. Add the potatoes and carrots to the boiling water, together with the sugar and garlic. Boil for 20 minutes on a moderate heat until the vegetables are tender.

Drain and mash vigorously, mix in the olive oil, chopped parsley, a squeeze of lemon juice, and seasoning to taste. Return to a low heat and stir gently for 2–3 minutes. Serve the mash with the gammon.

2 ounces (½ stick) butter

2 tablespoons olive oil

4 gammon steaks, each about 6 ounces

1 garlic clove, chopped

1 Spanish onion, finely chopped

1 eating apple, peeled, cored and diced

1 ounce (4 tablespoons) flour

18 fluid ounces (2 cups) dry cider

2 tablespoons Piccalilli
(see page 233, or bought)

1 teaspoon honey

4 sage leaves

1 teaspoon Dijon mustard

salt and pepper

½ lemon

¼ pint (⅔ cup) meat or vegetable broth

for the carrot & potato mash

4 large potatoes, quartered

2 large carrots, cut into chunks

1 teaspoon sugar

2 garlic cloves, peeled

2 tablespoons olive oil

a handful of chopped parsley

½ lemon

herb-wrapped beef
with brussels sprouts & pommes parmentier

Pour the olive oil into a large casserole dish and heat gently. Slice 1 of the garlic cloves into thin slivers and chop the other. Stud the beef fillet with the garlic slivers, season the fillet and seal it in the hot oil. When the fillet is nicely browned on all sides, remove and place on a plate to one side.

Pull the casserole off the heat and stir in the red onion, mushrooms, chopped garlic, carrot, and butter. Put the casserole dish back on to the heat and gently cook the vegetables for 3–4 minutes.

Lay all but 2 rashers of the bacon out in a row along your chopping board. Take the beef and baste it on all sides with the Dijon mustard and a tablespoon of horseradish. Now sprinkle the fillet with finely chopped herbs and place it on the bacon. Wrap the slices of bacon around the beef and tie securely at intervals with string. Place the wrapped and tied beef in the casserole, quickly seal the bacon on all sides and remove.

Pour the red wine into the casserole and boil to reduce by half. Add the beef or veal broth and reduce again by half. Turn the heat to the lowest possible setting, place the beef back in the casserole again and cook gently for 20 minutes, turning it once after 7–10 minutes. When it is cooked, pull to one side.

While the beef cooks, make the pommes parmentier: heat the olive oil in a large skillet, add the potato cubes, garlic, and chopped reserved bacon. Stir the potatoes occasionally until they are cooked to a golden brown. Finish with salt, pepper, a squeeze of lemon juice, and a handful of breadcrumbs (if you have them).

Cook the Brussels sprouts in gently boiling water for 4–6 minutes, until just tender, then drain. Return them to the pan, add the knob of butter, a pinch each of salt and pepper, and the balsamic vinegar. Put back on the heat for a couple of minutes to allow them to caramelize.

Serve the beef with the sprouts, potatoes, and a good dollop of horseradish.

2 tablespoons olive oil

2 garlic cloves

1 trimmed whole beef fillet, about 2 pounds

salt and pepper

1 red onion, chopped

2 ounces button mushrooms, or mixed wild mushrooms if available, chopped

1 carrot, finely chopped

2 ounces (½ stick) butter

8 ounces smoked bacon

1 tablespoon Dijon mustard

1 tablespoon creamed horseradish, plus lots more to serve

a large handful of chopped mixed fresh garden herbs, such as thyme, mint, rosemary, parsley

½ bottle of red wine

½ pint (1¼ cups) beef or veal broth

for the pommes parmentier

4 tablespoons olive oil

4 large potatoes, cut into small cubes

1 garlic clove, chopped

1 lemon

a handful of breadcrumbs (optional)

for the Brussels sprouts

1 pound Brussels sprouts

a knob of butter

1 tablespoon balsamic vinegar

seared pork fillet

with prosciutto, sage, & mustard, broiled apples, & red cabbage coleslaw

First prepare the coleslaw: mix all ingredients together in a large bowl, season to taste, cover and chill in the refridgerator.

Gently heat the olive oil in a large skillet, place the pork fillets in the pan and seal until light brown on both sides. Wrap each pork fillet in 2 slices of prosciutto and place to one side. Reheat the skillet and add the garlic, mustard, wine and vegetable broth, lemon juice, sage and salt and pepper to taste. Reduce by a half and leave to simmer. Put the prosciutto-wrapped pork back in the pan and cook gently for 10 minutes.

Prepare the apples: preheat a hot broiler, brush the apple slices with olive oil, then sprinkle with a pinch each of sugar and salt. Broil them until golden brown on both sides.

Serve the coleslaw and apples on the base of the plate. Slice the pork fillet and arrange on top. Finish with a spoonful of the pan juices and some sage leaves.

4 tablespoons olive oil

4 pork fillets, each about 4 ounces

8 slices of prosciutto

2 garlic cloves, finely chopped

2 tablespoons Dijon mustard

1 glass of dry white wine

½ pint (1¼ cups) vegetable broth

juice of 1 lemon

12 whole sage leaves

salt and pepper

for the red cabbage coleslaw

½ red cabbage, finely chopped

2 carrots, shredded

1 Spanish onion, finely chopped

1 garlic clove, finely chopped

2 tablespoons olive oil

juice of 1 lemon

4 tablespoons mayonnaise

salt and pepper

for the broiled apples

4 apples, cored and sliced

olive oil, for brushing

a pinch of sugar

Obviously, you can use 16 chicken portions for this dish. Thighs and drumsticks are best. Try to get free-range or corn-fed portions; they may be more expensive but they have so much more flavor.

provençale chicken
with olives, anchovies, & onion mash

2 chickens, each jointed into 8 pieces
4 garlic cloves, thinly sliced
1 tablespoon finely chopped fresh thyme
1 tablespoon finely chopped fresh marjoram
juice of 1 lemon
2 tablespoons olive oil

for the sauce
4 tablespoons olive oil
4 red onions, thinly sliced
6 garlic cloves, chopped
4 sprigs of thyme
5 basil leaves
6 sprigs of marjoram
21 ounces canned chopped tomatoes with their juice
½ bottle of dry white wine
30 small black olives, pitted
4 celery stalks
1 small jar or can of capers
1 small can of anchovies (1¾ ounces, about 6 fillets)
salt and pepper

for the mash
3 pounds potatoes, quartered
1 garlic clove, lightly crushed
4 ounces (1 stick) butter
4 tablespoons olive oil
2 bunches of scallions
¼ pint (⅔ cup) warmed milk

Serves 4–6

Preheat the oven to 350°F. Make the sauce: heat the oil in a saucepan and gently sweat the red onions, garlic, and herbs in it for 10 minutes. Add the remaining sauce ingredients (the anchovies will dissolve in the heat) and simmer for 15 minutes. Taste and adjust the seasoning.

While the sauce is busy simmering, prepare the chicken pieces. Mix the garlic with the herbs. Using a sharp knife, make small slits in the flesh of the chicken and push herb-covered slivers of garlic deep into the cuts. Rub the skin with lemon juice and season to taste with salt and pepper.

Heat the oil in a flameproof casserole dish and brown the chicken pieces all over. Pour over the hot sauce, cover and bake in the preheated oven for 20–30 minutes, until the chicken is cooked.

While the chicken cooks, make the mash: half-fill a saucepan with water (about 3½ pints), add salt, cover and bring to boil. Add the potatoes to the boiling water, together with the garlic. Boil for 20 minutes on a moderate heat until the potatoes are tender. Drain and mash vigorously, adding the butter, oil, scallions, milk and seasoning to taste.
Return to a low heat and stir gently for 2–3 minutes. Serve with the chicken.

grilled lamb
with cous cous & yogurt dressing

4 lamb neck fillets,
each about 4 ounces

2 tablespoons olive oil

1 garlic clove, chopped

4 tablespoons balsamic
vinegar

½ glass of red wine

4 sprigs of rosemary

½ pint (1¼ cups) meat broth

a pinch of sugar

salt and pepper

a good pinch of celery salt

a good pinch of dried oregano

juice of ½ lemon

2 handfuls of fine green beans

for the tzatsiki

½ cucumber

1 garlic clove, smashed into
a paste with the flat of a knife

salt

a bunch of mint, chopped

½ lemon

1 tablespoon olive oil

9 fl. oz. (1 cup) Greek yogurt

for the cous cous

3 ounces (½ cup) cous cous

2 ounces (½ cup) pine nuts,
toasted

2 handfuls of seedless raisins

a small bunch of flat-leaf
parsley, chopped

juice of 2 lemons and
shredded rind of 1

8 tablespoons olive oil

a pinch of ground cumin

Serves 2

First make the tzatsiki: chop the cucumber into small cubes, place in a strainer and allow to drain. In a large bowl, mix the ground garlic, a good pinch of salt, and one-third of the chopped mint. Add a squeeze of lemon juice and the olive oil, mix well and then add the yogurt, followed by the drained cucumber. Mix gently and chill in the fridge.

Trim any sinew from the lamb fillets. Heat 2 tablespoons of oil in a large saucepan and seal the lamb. Remove the fillets from the pan and place to one side. Add the garlic to the pan and quickly add the balsamic vinegar and red wine. Bring to a boil, then add the rosemary and half the remaining chopped mint. Now add the meat broth and sugar with salt and pepper to taste and allow to simmer until reduced by half.

While it simmers, dust the lamb fillets with celery salt and dried oregano and place in the simmering juices. Cover with a lid and cook gently for 5 minutes. Remove the lamb fillets and reduce the sauce by half, squeezing in the lemon juice.

Prepare the cous cous: soak the cous cous as per the packet instructions, then add the toasted pine nuts, raisins, chopped parsley, remaining chopped mint, the lemon juice and rind, olive oil, cumin, and salt and pepper to taste. Mix well.

While the cous cous soaks, cook the green beans in boiling salted water for 4–5 minutes until just tender. Drain well.

Slice each lamb fillet into pieces and place over the cous cous and green beans. Spoon over the lamb juices and finish with a big dollop of tzatsiki.

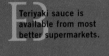

Teriyaki sauce is available from most better supermarkets.

crispy duck teriyaki
noodle salad

Preheat the oven to 400°F. Make the dressing: mix all the liquid ingredients together, then add the sliced garlic and ginger. Lightly score the duck fat and spoon one-third of the dressing over the duck.

Place a dry flameproof baking dish on the hob over a medium heat and seal the duck breasts, fat side first, then place the baking dish in the oven and cook for 8 minutes. Remove from the oven and allow to cool. Keep the oven on.

Once the duck is cool enough to handle, slice each breast into thin slices and then toss the slices in 2 more tablespoons of the teriyaki dressing. Put them back in the oven for a further 2 minutes to allow the dressing to caramelize slightly (a bit like sweet-and-sour pork).

Soak the noodles as per the instructions on the packet. Bring a saucepan of water to a boil and blanch the beans for 1 minute. Drain and add to the cooked noodles, then mix in the cilantro sprigs, shallots, and scallions. Add the slices of duck with the remaining dressing and mix well. Garnish with some more cilantro and serve.

2 whole free-range duck breasts

2 tablespoons teriyaki sauce

2 bunches of fine rice noodles (glass noodles)

4 ounces extra-fine green beans

20 sprigs of fresh cilantro, plus more to garnish

2 banana shallots, thinly sliced

4 scallions, thinly sliced

for the oriental teriyaki dressing

8 tablespoons teriyaki sauce

4 tablespoons soy sauce

6 tablespoons sesame oil

2 teaspoons clear honey

juice of 2 limes

4 garlic cloves, thinly sliced

1 inch piece of fresh ginger, shredded

goat cheese & vegetable millefeuille

Heat ½ inch of olive oil in a saucepan. Add the onion and garlic to the pan and cook gently until translucent. Add the red bell peppers and cook for 5 minutes, then add the zucchini, eggplant, and mushrooms. Cook gently for 20–25 minutes, stirring occasionally.

Add the tomatoes and cook for 5 minutes more. Then add the anchovy fillets and chopped black olives, and cook for a further 10–15 minutes, still on a low heat. Remove from the heat and pour the contents of the pan into a large bowl. Add the toasted pine nuts and a squeeze of lemon juice. Mix well, spoon on to plates and sprinkle with the basil and mixed leaves or arugula.

Preheat a hot broiler. Place the slices of goat cheese on an oiled baking sheet and whack under the broiler until golden brown. Put the cheese on top of the vegetables and salad.

olive oil, for frying
½ Spanish onion, chopped
1 garlic clove, chopped
2 red bell peppers, seeded and chopped
1 zucchini, cut into small chunks
2 eggplant, cut into small chunks
2 large flat-cap field mushrooms, finely chopped
4 beef tomatoes, seeded and chopped
2 anchovy fillets, chopped
a handful of pitted black olives
a handful of lightly toasted pine nuts
½ lemon
a handful of shredded basil
a bunch of mixed leaves or wild arugula leaves
4 thick slices from a goat cheese log

linguine marinara

Clean and debeard the mussels and clams, discarding any that are open and don't close when tapped.

Heat 5–6 tablespoons of olive oil in a large flameproof casserole. Add to this all the seafood except the anchovies and cook over a high heat for 3 minutes. Add ½ glass of the white wine and cook for a further 2 minutes. The mussels and clams will open, but discard any that don't. Remove and place in a bowl with the parsley and lemon rind.

Add the garlic, onion, carrots, and celery to the oil remaining in the casserole and cook for 4 minutes, stirring now and again. Add the anchovy fillets and cook for a further minute, then add the remaining wine and reduce by half. Add the fish broth and the puréed tomatoes, and cook gently for 30 minutes. Stir in all the seafood, then season to taste.

Towards the end of the sauce cooking time, bring a large saucepan of salted water to a boil, add the linguine and cook for 7 minutes or until al dente. Drain and add to the marinara sauce. Stir well, adding 2 more tablespoons of olive oil, and serve with finely shredded Parmesan.

4 ounces mussels in the shell

4 ounces clams
(fresh or drained canned)

about 4 fluid ounces (½ cup) olive oil

4 ounces cooked shrimp in the shell

4 cooked small crawfish in the shell

1 squid tube, cut across into rings

¼ bottle of dry white wine

1 pint (2½ cups) fish broth

a bunch of flat-leaf parsley, chopped

shredded rind and juice of 2 lemons

2 garlic cloves, chopped

1 red onion, chopped

2 carrots, chopped

2 celery stalks, chopped

2 anchovy fillets

1 14 ounce can of chopped
tomatoes, puréed

salt and pepper

7 ounces (1¾ cups) linguine

finely shredded Parmesan cheese,
to serve

Poured into a sterilized bottle and sealed, this cilantro teriyaki dressing can be kept for up to a week in the refrigerator and is wonderful with cooked duck, chicken wings, noodles, seafood, and just about anything!

fishcakes
teriyaki dressing & oriental salad

First make the cilantro teriyaki dressing: put the honey, garlic, ginger, lemon grass, and lime rind in a bowl, add the soy and teriyaki sauces, and blend together with a whisk. As the honey starts to blend with the other ingredients, begin to whisk in the sesame oil. Once all the oil is blended in, whisk in the lime juice and add the chopped cilantro.

Make the salad: cut the fennel into small wedges and put to blanch in a large saucepan of boiling salted water for 7 minutes. Cut each of the heads of bok choy into 4 chunks and add to the pan to blanch with the fennel for a further 3 minutes. Drain and allow to cool.

Put the blanched vegetables in a large bowl with the chopped cilantro leaves (keep the stems for later!) and beansprouts. Add the sugar, white wine vinegar, sesame oil, and 8 tablespoons of the teriyaki dressing. Toss and chill in refridgerator.

Make the fishcakes: lightly oil a baking sheet. Put the ginger in a food processor with the lime rind, chile, garlic, and the reserved cilantro stalks. Blend roughly. Cut the cod into chunks and add to blender with the coconut flakes and tomato purée. Mix to a thick paste.

Remove the mixture from the blender and put in a large bowl. Stir in the Japanese breadcrumbs. Mix with your fingers and shape into small balls about the size of a squash ball. Oil a baking sheet and the palms of your hands, then flatten the balls into small discs, place on the oiled baking sheet and chill in the refridgerator for 15–20 minutes to set. Put some flour in one shallow bowl, the egg in a second and the breadcrumbs in a third. Coat each fishcake well all over first in the flour, then in the egg, and finally in the breadcrumbs, shaking off any excess of each. Place them on a baking sheet as they are coated.

When required, cook the fishcakes in ¾ inch of hot vegetable oil, 5 or 6 at a time, in a large skillet over a moderate heat, for 3–4 minutes each side. As they are cooked, drain them on a paper towel and serve on top of the chilled oriental salad, garnished with a wedge of lime.

for the teriyaki dressing
2 tablespoons clear runny honey
1 garlic clove, finely chopped
1 teaspoon shredded fresh ginger
1 lemon grass stalk, smashed and finely chopped
finely shredded rind and juice of 2 limes
1½ tablespoons soy sauce
3 tablespoons teriyaki sauce
4 fluid ounces (½ cup) sesame oil
a bunch of fresh cilantro, finely chopped

for the salad
1 fennel bulb
salt
4 heads of bok choy
a bunch of fresh cilantro
2 ounces (1 cup) beansprouts
2 teaspoons sugar
2 tablespoons white wine vinegar
4 tablespoons sesame oil

for the fishcakes
vegetable oil, for frying and greasing
1 small piece of fresh ginger, shredded
finely shredded rind of 2 limes
1 red chile, seeded and chopped
2 small garlic cloves
2 pounds cod fillets, skinned and any bones removed
a handful of coconut flakes
1 level teaspoon tomato purée
2 handfuls of Japanese breadcrumbs, plus more for dusting
flour for dusting
1 egg, beaten
lime wedges, to serve

A pestle and mortar, if you have them, grind the fennel seeds well; if you don't have such kit, a pepper mill or rolling pin will do the job.

This is a great dish to make up and keep in the refridgerator for a day before cooking.

sea bass en papillote
with potato & bean salad

Rip off a 12 inch square sheet of aluminum foil, place it on a flat work surface, drizzle with olive oil and sprinkle with some seasoning. Place a sea bass fillet on the foil, squeeze over the juice of a tomato, and sprinkle with a quarter of the rosemary and ground fennel seeds. Drizzle over a teaspoon of the Pernod, followed by a teaspoon of olive oil. Finish with a teaspoon of crème fraîche, some salt and pepper and ½ an anchovy fillet. Fold the foil over gently, sealing the edges to create a loose parcel. Repeat with the remaining fillets to make 4 parcels in all. Place your parcels in the refridgerator to chill.

Cook the potatoes in boiling salted water for 8 minutes. In a bowl, mix the parsley, raw green beans, chopped onion and garlic, the rind and juice of the limes, the scallions, and the chiles. Drain the cooked potatoes and add straight to the bowl of chopped vegetables (the heat from the potatoes will slightly cook the beans and other veg). Add the white wine vinegar and 8 tablespoons of olive oil, then allow to sit until cool. Preheat the oven to 400°F.

Cook the sea bass fillets parcels in the preheated oven for 10 minutes. Remove and allow to rest for a minute or two, then serve with the well-mixed potato and bean salad.

about ¼ pint (⅔ cup) olive oil

salt and pepper

4 fillets of sea bass, each about 6 ounces

4 tomatoes

2 sprigs of rosemary, destalked and finely chopped

½ ounce fennel seeds, ground

4 teaspoons Pernod

9 fluid ounces (1 cup) crème fraîche

2 anchovy fillets, cut in half lengthwise

20 new potatoes, quartered lengthwise

a bunch of flat-leaf parsley, chopped

8 ounces fine green beans

1 red onion, chopped

2 garlic cloves, chopped

finely shredded rind and juice of 2 limes

2 scallions, chopped

2 red chiles, seeded and chopped

1 tablespoon white wine vinegar

risotto saganaki
with arugula & cucumber salad

Put the vegetable broth in a saucepan and bring to a boil. While the broth is heating, sauté the shrimp and finely chopped chile in 3 tablespoons of the olive oil until golden, then pull off the heat. Purée the canned tomatoes with a little oregano and the remaining olive oil, and place to one side.

Gently melt 1 stick of the butter in a large flameproof casserole and add the onion, celery, carrots and garlic. Sweat gently for 10 minutes until softened. Now add the Arborio rice and stir for 3 minutes. Pour in the white wine and cook, stirring from time to time, until the rice mixture becomes firm.

Slowly start to add the simmering vegetable broth to the rice, ⅔ cup at a time every 2–3 minutes, stirring occasionally. Once all the broth has been added, gently stir in the puréed tomatoes, then crumble in the feta cheese. Add the parsley followed by the cooked shrimp. Season to taste with salt and pepper.

Make the salad by tossing the arugula leaves and cucumber with the oil, lemon juice and seasoning to taste. Serve the risotto with the salad.

2 pints (5 cups) vegetable broth
2 ounces small peeled cooked shrimp
1 red chile, seeded and finely chopped
4 tablespoons olive oil
1 9 ounce can of tomatoes, drained
a good pinch of dried oregano
6 ounces (1½ sticks) butter
1 onion, finely chopped
4 whole celery stalks, finely chopped
2 carrots, finely chopped
3 garlic cloves, finely chopped
9 ounces (1 heaped cup) Arborio rice
½ bottle of good white wine
4 ounces feta cheese
salt and pepper

for the arugula & cucumber salad
3 ounces arugula leaves
1 cucumber, chopped
4 tablespoons olive oil
juice of 1 lemon

aegean pita pockets
with tzatsiki

This recipe is dedicated to my brother John, who used to rustle it up for a quick healthy lunch when we lived together – he was usually still eating it when he shot out of the door, heading back to work.

Trim all the fat off the pork chops and slice the meat into cubes about ¾ inch square. Put in a bowl with a squeeze of lemon juice, the olive oil, oregano, salt and pepper. Stir well, then tip into a skillet and fry for 5 minutes over a medium heat. When golden brown, leave the pan over the lowest possible heat and add the chopped peppers. Allow to cook gently for 5 minutes.

Meanwhile, cube the avocado, tomatoes, and feta, and mix together in a large bowl. Add the entire contents of skillet to the salad, then add the tzatsiki and mix well.

Give the pan a bit of a wipe and put back on the heat. Place the pita bread in the pan and warm through on each side. Cut a slit along the top edge of each pita and stuff with the mixture. Serve all 4 on a large plate. They should be cooked, stuffed, and eaten as soon as possible!

2 pork chops, each about 4 ounces
½ lemon
2 tablespoons olive oil
2 pinches of dried oregano
salt and pepper
1 red bell pepper, seeded and chopped
1 green bell pepper, seeded and chopped
1 avocado
6 tomatoes
7 ounces feta cheese
Tzatsiki (page 44)
4 pita breads

Often broiling or toasting pita makes it biscuit-hard...not a good thing. The best way to heat pita is to drizzle it lightly with oil and warm gently in a skillet for 20–30 seconds on either side. Do this only after you've made up all your ingredients, then slice the side of the pita to stuff it with filling.

zucchini & artichoke frittata

Frittata is an Italian style of omelet – half French and half Spanish, whisking the eggs quite ferociously like a French omelet and cooking slowly and gently like a Spanish omelet.

Make a herb seasoning by finely chopping the thyme leaves and mixing them with a pinch of salt and a twist of pepper. Gently heat the olive oil in a 10 inch skillet, add the sliced onion and garlic and gently cook until softened. Add the sliced artichokes, cannellini beans, and shredded zucchini to the pan and cook gently for 3–4 minutes. Add the thyme seasoning, pull the pan off the heat and allow to cool for 2–3 minutes.

Break the eggs into a mixing bowl and beat vigorously. Pour the warm ingredients into the beaten eggs and fold together.

Return the pan to the heat and pour in the contents of the bowl. Stir gently with a spatula for 2 minutes, until the frittata starts to set. Cook on the lowest heat possible, as you would a Spanish omelet, until firm.

Place a plate over the pan and flip the frittata onto it. Dust with Parmesan cheese and serve with a tomato and mixed leaf salad.

4 sprigs of thyme

salt and pepper

6 tablespoons olive oil

1 red onion, thinly sliced

1 garlic clove, thinly sliced

5 artichoke hearts (preferably fresh, see page 36, but drained canned will do), sliced

1 14 ounce can of cannellini beans, drained and washed

1 large zucchini (about 7 ounces), shredded

5 eggs

1 ounce (½ cup) Parmesan cheese

tomato and mixed leaf salad, to serve

When cooking for a dinner party I find it much easier to prepare as much food in advance as I can. I also favor dishes that can be presented on large plates to be put on the table at the same time, with everyone helping themselves, rather in the way you might eat Sunday lunch or Oriental food. This is a relaxed, sociable way of eating that also enables you to spend a lot more of the evening with your friends, instead of relaying back and forth to and from the kitchen, to the point that you forget what you are running in and out for.

To cook like this requires a slightly different philosophy, and an element of organization. For instance – and you've probably heard this before – once all your food is prepared, clean up! Cooking is one of those crafts where everything comes together at the last minute, so why try putting it together three times throughout the evening when you can do all three at once, before your guests are even sitting down.

dining

Of the two types of foie gras available, duck or goose, personally I prefer duck foie gras. When slicing foie gras, first dip your knife in hot water each time you slice. This helps ensure a clean easy slice.

ade's foie gras

The reason I dedicate this dish to my mate Ade (pronounced 'ah-day' rather than 'aid') is that, after his success on the silver screen appearing in *Snatch* as Tyrone, his culinary experience expanded to fine dining across the globe and, one night out, he experienced foie gras for the first time. He later asked, half jokingly, if I could make it for him. Needless to say, I did, and once I had he declared it was the finest foie gras he'd ever tasted, and that he could eat it daily on toast. I cautioned him that if eaten daily, even if his pocket could afford it, his waistline couldn't.

Chill a 8 x 4 inch terrine mold in the freezer. On a piece of cardboard, measure out a 7 x 3 inch rectangle. Cut this shape out with scissors, wrap it in plastic wrap and place it to one side. Cut the foie gras widthwise into slices about 2 inches thick. Lay the slices flat on a baking sheet and brush with brandy and port if using it, then sprinkle with salt and pepper.

Place a large skillet on a moderate heat and, once the pan is hot, place the pieces of foie gras in it and cook for 30 seconds on each side, turning with a palette knife. Only cook 5 slices of foie gras at a time, ensuring each is properly done. The cooked slices should be a good brown. Each time you have cooked a batch of foie gras, pour off any excess juices into a heatproof jug or container. Once they are cooked, place the slices back on the tray and put the baking sheet in the refrigerator.

Remove the terrine mold from the freezer, brush all the insides with the reserved juices from cooking the foie gras and put the mold back in the freezer for 3 minutes. Repeat this whole process again twice to build up layers of solid fat inside the mold.

Now remove the foie gras from the refrigerator (from this point you must work quite quickly), remove the terrine mold from the freezer and arrange the slices of foie gras evenly in layers in the terrine mold, fitting each piece snugly against the other standing in rows and seasoning each layer as you go. Pour any remaining cooking juices over the top and place back in the refrigerator for 30 minutes.

Take the chilled terrine out of the refrigerator, put it on a tray, and place the piece of cardboard on top of the terrine. Push it down and place a brick, or something of similar weight and size, on top to weight it down. Put the whole thing back in the refrigerator and chill now for a minimum of 4 hours – the longer the better, anything up to two days.

Make the chutney: peel and chop the kiwi fruit, and finely chop the onion and garlic. In a medium-sized saucepan, very gently cook the onion in 1 tablespoon of olive oil over a low heat until softened. Remove the pan from heat and add the chopped kiwi fruit and sugar.

2 lobes of foie gras

2 tablespoons brandy

2 tablespoons white port or use more brandy)

salt and pepper

toasted bread or brioche, to serve

for the chutney

5 kiwi fruits

1 Spanish onion

2 garlic cloves

1 tablespoon olive oil

4 ounces (½ cup) superfine sugar

2 tablespoons white wine vinegar

for the sauce

½ glass of red wine

9 fluid ounces (1 cup) veal broth

Bring back to the heat and allow the sugar to melt into the mix. Add the vinegar and bring to a boil, then simmer for 30–40 minutes and remove from the heat. Immediately pour the chutney into a sterilized jam jar and place the lid on. As it cools, a vacuum will be created at the top of the jar, enabling you to store the chutney in the refridgerator and use as required.

Just before serving the foie gras, make the sauce: bring the red wine to a boil in a saucepan and reduce by half. Pour in the veal broth and reduce by three-quarters. Pull to one side. Season.

Finally, take a dish towel and run it under hot water. Take the terrine out of the refridgerator, remove the weight and the cardboard lid and wrap the hot towel around the terrine dish, including the base. The warmth of the towel will loosen the terrine and stop it sticking when you turn it out. Hold a palette knife under hot water and very gently run the knife around the edges of the foie gras. Place a serving dish over the terrine and remove the dish towel. Turn the terrine and serving plate over together; the foie gras should slip easily from the mold.

To serve, cut the foie gras into slices about 1 inch thick, place on toasted bread or brioche, with a spoonful of chutney and a cordon of sauce. Season and tuck in. A bit of long-winded procedure, but the taste is well worth it.

Traditionally sauce au poivre is served with beef; you could use the recipe here with beef, lamb, and game, but I particularly like my sauce au poivre with pork chops.

pork chop au poivre
with apple mash

Quite often meat dishes are eaten with either fruit or wine/vinegar sauces. The reason for this primarily – other than it tasting good – is that these aid the digestion of the meat. You can also combine vegetables with fruit to create new flavors.

Strain off the liquid from the peppercorns for the sauce au poivre into a mixing bowl and place the peppercorns to one side. Add a tablespoon of oil and a twist of black pepper to the strained juice and then place the pork chops and kidney into the mixing bowl. Cover and put in the refridgerator to marinate.

Make the sauce au poivre: melt the butter with the oil in a medium-sized saucepan and add the carrot, onion, and garlic. Cook over a gentle heat until softened, then add 4 teaspoons of the reserved peppercorns to the pan and cook for 2–3 minutes more. Remove the pan from the heat and add the brandy, then return to the heat and simmer gently until that is reduced by half. Add the red wine and reduce in the same way. Finally add the broth and reduce by two-thirds. Pull the pan off the heat and leave, allowing all the flavors to infuse. Season with salt and pepper, and keep warm.

Make the apple mash: melt the butter in a large saucepan, add the garlic and cook for a minute over a gentle heat, then add the apples, vinegar, sugar, lemon juice, cinnamon, and milk. Continue to cook gently for 30 minutes, stirring occasionally. Meanwhile, boil the potatoes in a large saucepan of salted water for around 30 minutes. Drain and allow to cool. Put the potatoes back in the drained saucepan and, on a low heat, cook out as much of the moisture as possible. While you are doing this, begin to mash the potatoes and slowly start to add the apple mix. If the mash becomes too stiff (depending on how starchy your potatoes are), drizzle in a little olive oil. Once all the apples are in and mashed, pull the mash off the heat and place to one side. Keep warm.

Cook the pork chops: preheat the broiler to high. Remove the pork chops from the pepper juice, pat dry and place on the broiler sheet. Grill for 5 minutes on one side and 3 minutes on the other. Remove the broil tray, place a sage leaf on top of each chop, followed by a slice of kidney, and broil for a further 3 minutes.

Remove and place the chops on a large serving plate, pour over the sauce au poivre and serve with a bowl of apple mash. These go very well with braised broccoli and peas, or a tomato salad.

1 tablespoon olive oil

salt and pepper

4 pork chops, each about 7 ounces

1 pork kidney, sliced into 4 pieces

4 sage leaves

for the sauce au poivre

1 4 ounce can of green peppercorns

2 ounces (½ stick) butter

1 tablespoon olive oil

1 carrot, chopped

1 large onion, chopped

1 garlic clove, chopped

4 tablespoons brandy

1 glass of red wine

1 pint (2½ cups) beef broth

for the apple mash

2 ounces (½ stick) unsalted butter

1 garlic clove, finely chopped

2 large cooking apples peeled, cored, and thinly sliced

1 teaspoon white wine vinegar

½ level teaspoon sugar

juice of ½ lemon

a pinch of ground cinnamon

4 tablespoons milk

4 large potatoes, peeled and quartered

about 4 tablespoons olive oil

medallions of beef
with madeira, foie gras, & truffle oil

First make the apple röstis: peel the potatoes and apple, then shred into a colander. Squeeze the shredded potato and apple to remove as much water as possible (use your hands) – the drier the better. Add nutmeg, salt and pepper and mix well.

Heat 2 tablespoons of olive oil and ½ ounce of butter gently in a 6 inch skillet. Add a large serving spoonful of mixture to the pan over a moderate heat. Mold the potato to fill the base of the pan by pushing it down firmly. Cook over moderate heat for 4–5 minutes until golden and lightly crisp on the underside. Then turn the rösti over, press it down again and cook for a further 4–5 minutes. Remove and allow to rest on paper towels. Repeat to make 3 more.

Once the röstis are cooked and cool, using a 4 inch round cutter, cut each rösti into discs (trimmings can be put into the cutter to mold more discs). Place the discs on a lightly oiled sheet of aluminum foil on a baking sheet.

Wipe the skillet clean, cut the beef fillet into 8 equal slices (2 medallions per person). Heat the pan, add the oil and, when that is smoking, seal the beef fillets for about 1 minute on each side. Remove and place 2 on each of the röstis, then allow to cool. Once cooled, chill in the refridgerator until required.

Make the Madeira Sauce: add the chopped shallots and garlic to the pan with the oil, and reduce the heat to medium. Cook, stirring, until softened but not burned. Take off the heat and add the glass of Madeira, then reduce the heat and allow the Madeira to simmer gently until it has reduced by half. Add the beef broth to the pan and again allow to cook gently until reduced by half. Remove the pan from heat, season and place to one side.

When ready to serve: preheat the oven to 425°F. Slice the foie gras into 4 pieces and place a clean skillet over full heat. Using a palette knife, place the foie gras in the heated pan and seal it on both sides very quickly. Once sealed, place each slice of foie gras on a plate. Take the sheet of röstis and beef and put them in the oven for 5 minutes. Mix the juices left in the foie gras pan, with the truffle oil, balsamic vinegar and a twist of pepper. Dress the arugula leaves with these juices. Remove the medallions and röstis from the oven, put them on the plates and top with the slices of foie gras. Sprinkle arugula around the beef and finally spoon 2–3 tablespoons of the Madeira sauce on each plate.

1½ pounds beef fillet
1 tablespoon olive oil
7 ounces fresh foie gras
4 teaspoons truffle oil
1 teaspoon balsamic vinegar
4 handfuls of arugula leaves

for the apple röstis

2 potatoes
1 cooking apple
a pinch of freshly shredded nutmeg
salt and pepper
8 tablespoons olive oil, plus more for greasing
2 ounces (½ stick) butter

for the Madeira sauce

4 shallots, finely chopped
1 garlic clove, finely chopped
1 tablespoon olive oil
1 glass of Madeira
1 pint (2½ cups) beef broth

crispy roast duck
with artichoke mash & beet salad

Friends tell me they don't like cooking duck, as it ends up being fatty and a little bit tough. To achieve less thick, tough fat involves either steaming or boiling the duck before roasting. For the finest results, you need to roast your duck hanging upright. When buying for our restaurant in Soho I was lucky enough to track down an old 1950s oven, perfect for hanging ducks in to cook. I have to say it's the finest cooker I've ever used. I don't have one at home, however, and don't suppose you do either. If you follow the duck preparation below, though, your duck will be crisp and delicious. If you're a game lover, then you can eat wild duck in season, which involves a completely different method of cooking to that used in this dish. Wild duck is also not as readily available as farmed duck.

Place your duck in a large saucepan, breast side down, and cover it completely with water. Add the bay leaf. Strip the herbs leaves from their stalks and put to one side; add the stalks to the pan. Cover and bring to a boil. (You must be careful not to let the boiling water overflow, as it's full of fat that could catch fire.) When it is boiling, reduce to a steady simmer. After the duck has been simmering for 20 minutes, drain carefully in a colander, pouring the duck broth into a separate pan. Allow the duck to cool, then place it on a chopping board.

Preheat the oven to 400°F, setting the oven shelf as low as possible. Chop the herb leaves finely, as well as 1 garlic clove. Blend these together with a pinch of salt into a paste. Now cut small slits widthwise across both of the duck breasts and legs, at 1 inch intervals. Drizzle the duck lightly with olive oil and rub the herb and garlic paste all over the skin. Place the duck in a roasting pan and if you have a trivet use it now (if not, 3 raw carrots, or a couple of old serving spoons will do). Place the trivet (or carrots or spoons) beneath the duck to allow a flow of hot air under the duck, which will help it to crisp up. Place the duck to one side for at least 30 minutes to allow it to absorb the herb marinade.

Once it has marinated, put the duck in the oven and roast until golden brown, about 40 minutes.

While the duck cooks, make the mash: prepare the artichokes by bringing a large saucepan of salted water to a boil. If using globe artichokes, remove the stalks and

You can buy cooked beets in vac-packs, but cooking it yourself from raw gives a stronger and fresher taste, and the process is as easy as boiling potatoes. Shredded raw beets have a lovely nutty flavor that works really well in mixed salads, also adding its dramatic color and crunchy texture.

for the duck

1 large duck

1 bay leaf

a bunch of fresh rosemary

2 sprigs of fresh thyme

1 garlic clove

a really good pinch of salt

1 tablespoon olive oil

¼ pint (⅔ cup) red wine

for the artichoke mash

2 pounds Jerusalem artichokes, if available, or 6 globe artichokes

2 pounds (about 8) potatoes, peeled and quartered

4 tablespoons olive oil

1 garlic clove, chopped

a bunch of flat-leaf parsley (about ⅔ ounce), chopped

juice of 1 lemon

place the artichokes in the boiling water, then allow to boil for 20 minutes. Drain and allow to cool, then remove all the leaves and scrape the furry choke from the heart. If using Jerusalem artichokes, peel and boil the artichokes for 10 minutes. Drain.

While the artichokes are cooking, bring another large saucepan of salted water to a boil. Cook the potatoes in the boiling water for 20 minutes. Drain well and add the olive oil, the garlic and parsley to the pan. Put over a low heat and cook gently for 5 minutes. Then add the lemon juice and the cooked artichokes and potatoes, and mash together thoroughly. Pull to one side.

To make the beet salad: put the beets in a large skillet and cover with water. Add the balsamic vinegar and bring to a slow simmer. When all the liquid has been absorbed, the beets will be cooked, and the vinegar will have caramelized around the beets. Place the pan to one side.

Bring the pan of duck broth back to a boil, skimming the duck fat off the surface. Add the red wine and reduce by two-thirds. Once the duck is cooked, remove it from the oven and put it on a chopping board. Remove the trivet, carrots or spoons and pour off the fat from the roasting pan. Put the roasting pan back on the hob over a medium-to-low heat and add the reduced duck broth. Bring to a boil, stir and reduce the heat to a simmer.

Cut the duck into 8 pieces, 2 from each of the legs and 2 from the breast. Place the duck pieces on a large warmed serving dish and pour the gravy over it. Gently re-heat the beets and mash, if necessary. Serve the duck with the warm beets dressed with the olive oil and sprinkled with the basil, together with the artichoke mash.

for the beet salad

4 large beets, peeled and cubed

1 tablespoon balsamic vinegar

3 tablespoons olive oil

a pinch of shredded basil leaves

spatchcock chicken
with garlic, mustard, & sage stuffing & slow-cooked zucchini with hasselback potatoes

First prepare the zucchini: place in a colander and sprinkle with salt. Mix the salt in and leave them to stand for 30 minutes. This allows the moisture to be drawn out of the zucchini, intensifying their taste.

Then prepare the potatoes: cut them in half lengthwise and soak them in a bowl or saucepan of cold water for 20–30 minutes to remove some of the starch.

Prepare the chicken: preheat the oven to 425°F. Place the chicken on a chopping board and, with a large heavy knife, remove the central backbone with one firm vertical chop on each side. Once removed, turn the chicken over and push it flat. Remove the rib bones. You should now have one flattened piece of chicken, skin side down.

Make the stuffing: bring 1 pint (2½ cups) of water to a boil and add to it the garlic broken into cloves, still with their skins on. Boil for 20 minutes. Remove from the heat and drain. When cool enough to handle, peel the cloves. Finely chop the sage and put in a bowl, then mash it together with the garlic, mustard, salt, oil, and lemon juice.

Carefully push your fingers in a sweeping motion between the skin and breast of the chicken to create a pocket and gently spoon in the stuffing, secure the skin with a cocktail stick. Drizzle oil over the skin and season. Roast for 70 minutes.

Prepare the Hasselback potatoes: drain the potatoes, and make slits close together along each half, like a loaf of sliced bread but still connected at the base. Put the oil in a deep roasting pan, sprinkle in the paprika and some salt, and mix together. Gently heat on the stove. Add the potatoes, sliced side down, and cook over moderate heat for 2 minutes, turn and cook briefly on the other side. Place in the oven 30 minutes after the bird goes in and cook for 45 minutes.

Cook the zucchini: rinse and shake dry. Add the oil and garlic to a large saucepan and cook gently until soft. Add the zucchini, turn the heat up to full and cook for 5 minutes, stirring continuously. Now add the mint and parsley, stir for 2 minutes, reduce the heat and add the wine and a squeeze of lemon juice. Turn the heat to very low and cook gently for 40 minutes. When ready to serve, add pepper to taste but not salt.

Serve everything in large dishes, with wedges of lemon.

1 free-range chicken, about 4 pounds
lemon wedges, to serve

for the zucchini
2 pounds zucchini, cut into smallish chunks
salt
4 tablespoons olive oil
3 garlic cloves, chopped
a bunch of mint (about ½ ounce), chopped
a bunch of flat-leaf parsley (¾ ounce), chopped
½ glass of white wine
a squeeze of lemon juice

for the Hasselback potatoes
4 large potatoes
4 tablespoons olive oil
½ teaspoon paprika
a pinch of salt

for the stuffing
1 whole head of garlic
a bunch of sage leaves
1 tablespoon Dijon mustard
salt and pepper
1 tablespoon olive oil
juice of ½ lemon

pan-fried calves' liver
with gin & lime sauce, sweet potato, & artichoke gratin

Liver is one of my favorite dishes, especially when I am feeling a bit down in the dumps, as it's packed with iron and really picks you up. This accompanying sauce is a traditional old English recipe, and the two work wonderfully together. The gratin lifts the palate and complements the strong taste of liver.

First make the sauce: put a large saucepan on a gentle heat, add to it the olive oil and butter, followed by the shallots and garlic. Gently cook these over a moderate heat until translucent. Stir in the lime rind and parsley, add the gin, increase the heat to moderate-to-hot and bring to a boil. Once boiling, stir in the marmalade, lime juice and mustard, followed by the broth. Bring to a boil again, reduce the heat to moderate and allow to reduce by half. Pull the pan from the heat, add the Worcestershire sauce, a pinch of salt, and a twist of pepper, then place to one side.

Make the gratin: fill a mixing bowl with cold water and add the juice of half the lemon (this is for soaking the peeled artichokes, to prevent them discoloring while you're preparing the potatoes). In a large saucepan, bring about 3½ pints (8 cups) of water to a boil. Using a bread knife, trim the leaves of the artichokes down to the hearts, then cut the hearts into quarters and cut these in half again. Using a small sharp knife, remove any hairy choke from the artichoke hearts. Place the artichoke wedges in the lemon water. Peel the sweet potatoes and cut them widthways into discs about ¾ inch thick.

Add the sweet potatoes to the boiling water and blanch for 4 minutes, remove them with a slotted spoon and place them to one side. Repeat this blanching process with the artichokes, again for 4 minutes. Keep the liquid on a boil, as you have made a basic vegetable broth. Add to this broth any parsley stalks and artichoke leaves, and continue boiling for a further 10 minutes.

While this boils, heat the olive oil and butter in a large skillet, add the chopped onion and garlic, and cook very gently over the lowest heat possible until softened. Put the artichokes and sweet potatoes into the pan and increase the heat to moderate. Stir well and add the white wine, which should immediately boil off and reduce by half. Add a couple of ladlefuls of vegetable broth, just enough to cover the vegetables and turn the heat down to simmer. Cook for 10 minutes, season and pour all the vegetables, into a warmed oven dish.

Although pan-fried liver is traditionally first sliced as thinly as possible, when using good-quality calves' liver try to have it sliced about ¾ inch thick, as this makes it easier to ensure that it's pink inside when cooked. (When liver is cooked pink, it means that it is still cooked and not raw – when it's raw it's red inside.) Even if you like your liver well done, a slightly thicker cut makes it less leathery.

You can also easily freeze the gin and lime sauce in an ice cube tray, then use a cube or two each time you fancy it; gin & lime sauce is pretty fantastic with any offal dish.

8 slices of calves' liver, each about 2 ounces and ¾ inch thick

3 tablespoons olive oil

for the gin & lime sauce

1 tablespoon olive oil

1 ounce (2 tablespoons) butter

2 shallots, finely chopped

1 garlic clove, finely chopped

finely shredded rind and juice of 1 lime

a small bunch of flat-leaf parsley, chopped

2 tablespoons gin

1 teaspoon marmalade

1 teaspoon English mustard

½ pint (1¼ cups) beef broth

1 teaspoon Worcestershire sauce

salt and pepper

At this point, gently re-heat the gin sauce (liver must be served as soon as it is cooked, which doesn't take long at all). Preheat the broiler to full and preheat a griddle pan (or, if you don't have one, a skillet) until smoking. Take the pieces of liver and lay them out on a chopping board. Pat dry with paper towel (this ensures that the liver won't stick to the pan) and drizzle a little olive oil over them, then sprinkle with a little salt.

Squeeze the juice of the remaining ½ lemon over the gratin and then sprinkle with the Parmesan cheese, breadcrumbs, and some seasoning. Flash it under the broiler for not more than a minute.

Cook the pieces of liver on the griddle pan for 1 minute on each side and serve. I like to put all the liver on a large plate, the gin sauce in a warmed jug, and bring to the table with the gratin in the dish.

Another very simple way to finish liver once cooked on both sides is to add 2 tablespoons of balsamic vinegar to the pan – the balsamic vinegar will start to caramelize around the liver in seconds. Remove the liver from the pan and melt a dollop of crème fraîche in the pan, then pour this over the liver. Alternatively, chop the liver and pan-fry it in olive oil until nut brown. Add 2 tablespoons of balsamic vinegar, allow it to caramelize, then add half a ladleful of beef broth and 1 ounce of butter. Stir vigorously, season and serve.

for the gratin

1 lemon

4 globe artichokes

4 sweet potatoes

1 tablespoon olive oil

1 ounce (2 tablespoons) butter

½ Spanish onion, chopped

1 garlic clove, chopped

1 glass of white wine

about 1 glass of vegetable broth

1 ounce (½ cup) Parmesan cheese

1 ounce (2½ tablespoons) breadcrumbs

seared tuna
with chile, cilantro, & lime dressing

Grind the coriander seeds to a fine powder. Mix together well with a pinch of salt and the lime rind, then pour out onto a flat baking sheet. Cut the tuna loin lengthwise into quarters, so you have 4 fillets. Roll each fillet in the coriander seed mix.

Now lightly smear a large skillet with about 1 teaspoon of vegetable oil and place over a high heat until the pan is smoking. Add the tuna fillets to the hot pan one at a time, and cook until all the sides are sealed and blackened. Once this is done, place the fillets on a flat dish and put them in the fridge.

Make the dressing: put the ginger, chiles and garlic in a bowl and mash to a pulp (if you have a pestle and mortar, now's the time to use it; if not, the end of a rolling pin makes a good masher). Once pulped, add the juice from the limes and pour all these ingredients into a medium-sized mixing bowl, together with the vegetable oil, and mix well. Stir in the soy sauce and cilantro. Allow the dressing to rest, to enable all the flavors to infuse.

Remove the tuna from the fridge and cut each fillet into thin slices. Lay the slices out on a large serving plate (as you would carpaccio), spoon over two-thirds of the dressing, cover and chill until you are ready to serve. This recipe goes very well with arugula and bean salad, but whichever salad you choose, coat it with the remaining dressing.

4½ ounces coriander seeds

salt

finely shredded rind of 4 limes
(plus the juice for the dressing)

2¼ pounds fresh tuna loin

1 teaspoon vegetable oil

for the chile, cilantro, & lime dressing

4 inch piece of fresh ginger, peeled and finely shredded

4 red chiles, seeded and finely chopped

2 garlic cloves, chopped

6 tablespoons vegetable oil

2 tablespoons soy sauce

a bunch of fresh cilantro, roughly chopped (stalks and all)

roast turbot
with thyme gremolata & braised greens

The cheeks of the turbot are a true delicacy, the ancient Romans indulged in them for their aphrodisiac qualities.

The gremolata, an Italian combination of salt, lemon rind and thyme, really cuts through the butter and helps to crisp up the outer skin of the fish.

Without a doubt, turbot is one of the most delicious fish in the world. Although our cousins in the southern hemisphere regularly brag about their fish, to my mind nothing beats cold-water Atlantic fish, especially turbot. The fish grows to an enormous size but is at its tastiest when it weighs in at about 2–3 pounds. Because it is in high demand in Europe – where people are quite happy to pay the very high prices – turbot is not often seen in supermarkets, so a visit to your fish merchant is in order here. I recently cooked this dish for some friends, and they later called me for the recipe, so sorry I'm a bit late guys, but here it is.

Trim the turbot with a pair of sharp scissors, cutting away the outer fin around the fish. Pat the fish dry with some paper towel then, using a sharp knife, cut deep incisions about 2 inches apart across the brown side of the fish.

Prepare the gremolata: strip the thyme leaves from the stalks, discard the stalk, and finely chop the leaves. In a large bowl, mix them with the salt and lemon rind. Spread this dry marinade all over the brown side of the fish, rubbing it into the slits. Place the fish on a chopping board or tray that fits into your refridgerator and chill.

Prepare the vegetables (it's very important to serve this dish quickly once it's cooked, so you need to make sure that all your vegetables are ready to go when half the fish is done): cut the sugar snaps in half, and place to one side. Cut the French beans into pieces and place to one side.

Place a deep skillet over a moderate heat and add the olive oil, onion and garlic. Stir in the French beans, add a squeeze of lemon juice and ½ pint (1¼ cups) of water. Bring to a boil and then turn down the heat to a low simmer. After 15 minutes, add the sugar snaps and cook for a further 15 minutes until all the water has been absorbed. Pull to one side, lightly season with salt and pepper.

1 whole turbot, tail and all, about 2½–3 pounds

¼ pint (⅔ cup) olive oil

18 of cherry tomatoes

4 garlic cloves

½ glass of white wine

9 fluid ounces vegetable broth

lemon wedges, to serve

for the thyme gremolata

a large bunch of fresh thyme

3 tablespoons rock salt or Maldon salt

finely shredded rind of 4 lemons

for the chile potatoes

16 new potatoes

salt

5 tablespoons olive oil

2 teaspoons vinegar (malt, red wine, white wine, whichever you have)

a bunch of mint, finely chopped

2 good pinches of slivered dried chiles

for the braised greens

1 pound sugar snap peas

1 pound French beans

4 tablespoons olive oil

1 Spanish onion, finely chopped

1 garlic clove, finely chopped

a squeeze of lemon juice

salt and pepper

While the vegetables are cooking, preheat the oven to 400°F and prepare the potatoes: blanch them in boiling salted water for 4 minutes, drain and allow to cool. When cool, cut them into slices about 1½ inches thick. Heat the olive oil in a large skillet or wok and add the slices of potato. Fry, tossing, until golden-brown on all sides. Remove from heat and shake and strain, then pour out on to a paper towel. Once all the excess oil is drained off, add the potatoes back to the pan and place to one side. You can reheat them gently on the stove and season them just before serving.

To cook the turbot: pour the olive oil into a deep baking pan and place on the stove over a low heat. This will stop the fish sticking to the pan when you're baking it. Gently place the fish, white side down, in the warmed olive oil, then slightly move the fish around to seal it. Add the cherry tomatoes and garlic cloves, and cook in the oven for 25 minutes.

While the fish is cooking, chop the mint and gently reheat the potatoes on the stove to crisp them up. Pour them into a bowl, add the vinegar, mint, and chiles, and stir well. Put your serving plate for the turbot into the bottom of the oven. Quickly warm the vegetables through and put in a warmed serving dish.

Remove the turbot from the oven and, using at least one or two fish slices or spatulas, place it on the preheated dish. Now reduce the juices, tomatoes and garlic in the baking pan by placing it on the stove and bringing it to a boil, adding the white wine and the vegetable broth, and scraping up any fish and vegetable remains off the bottom. Pass the gravy through a strainer into a jug and serve with the fish, potatoes and vegetables, with lemon wedges on the side. The fish should slide easily from the bone, and is best done at the table so everyone can muck in.

Scoring the skin of the
snapper allows it to
absorb the marinade
more readily, lets the
heat through to the
flesh and stops the fish
from curling as it cooks.

If you get your cilantro
with the roots attached,
clean them well and
use them in the
marinade too.

slow-roast red snapper
sweet potato bubble & squeak, & greens

Combine all the marinade ingredients together. Take the cilantro leaves from their stalks in one slice and reserve. Then finely chop the cilantro stalks and add them to the marinade. With a sharp knife, lightly score the skin side of the fish at 1 inch intervals. Mix the marinade well and add the snapper fillets. Turn gently to coat well.

Make the bubble & squeak: bring 2 large saucepans of salted water to a boil. In one, boil the cabbage for 30 minutes and then drain well; in the other, cook the ordinary potatoes for 10 minutes, then add the sweet potatoes and cook for a further 10 minutes. Drain. Put the potatoes back in the saucepan and dry them out over a gentle heat, while mashing them thoroughly. Add the cabbage, mix and keep mashing until the potatoes and cabbage are well blended. Now add the flour and a good pinch of salt and pepper. Mix well, pull from heat and leave to cool.

Dust a work surface lightly with flour, and scoop out golfball-sized handfuls of potato mixture. Using your hands or a palette knife, shape these into small patties. Lightly grease a baking sheet that fits in your refridgerator and, once you have made 8 patties, chill for about 30 minutes.

When ready to serve: preheat the oven to 300°F. Steam your selected vegetables for 5 minutes, then toss lightly in olive oil and pepper. Gently heat a little butter and a couple of tablespoons of olive oil in a skillet and cook the bubble and squeak patties until browned on both sides. Place them on a baking sheet, then put them in the oven on the lowest shelf to keep warm while you cook the fish.

Cover your broiler pan with a large piece of aluminum foil and preheat the broiler to moderate. Remove the snapper from the refridgerator. Spoon a little marinade on to the foil, place the fillets on the foil, skin side up, and cover them with a little more of the marinade, then dust with a small pinch of sugar. Place under the broiler and cook for 6–8 minutes on one side only (due to the reflective heat of the foil, you do not need to turn the fillets over).

Serve the bubble and squeak covered with vegetables and a piece of snapper on top. Spoon over any remaining marinade and serve with a chunk of lime.

a bunch of fresh cilantro
4 pieces of red snapper fillet, each about 7 ounces
a small pinch of sugar
chunky lime wedges, to serve

for the marinade
1 glass of dry sherry
finely shredded rind and juice of 2 limes
1 tablespoon soy sauce
¼ pint (⅔ cup) vegetable oil
a dash of Tabasco sauce
1 teaspoon shredded fresh ginger
1 teaspoon sugar
a pinch of dried slivered chiles

for the sweet potato bubble & squeak
salt and pepper
10 ounce white cabbage, shredded
14 ounces potatoes, peeled and quartered
10 ounces sweet potatoes, peeled and quartered
1 tablespoon all-purpose flour, plus more for dusting
a little butter
2 tablespoons olive oil

suggested vegetables to serve
carrots, white radish
olive oil, to dress

pan-fried skate
with bacon, anchovy, tomato, & caper sauce, fennel gratin

Strong flavors complement this fish extremely well and skate is traditionally served poached with beurre noir, a sauce made using burnt butter, vinegar, parsley and capers. Similarly, with this recipe it is the combination of the strong and sharp flavors of anchovy, capers, and lemon, combined with the sweetness of tomato and fennel that works so well. Simple but delicious...

First make the sauce: heat the olive oil in a large skillet and add the bacon and anchovy fillets. Cook over a moderate heat for 3–4 minutes, then add the capers, parsley, and lemon rind. Cook for a further minute, then add the white wine and reduce by half. Add the tomato juice and cook gently over a low heat for about 30 minutes. Season.

Make the gratin: preheat the oven to 350°F. Bring a large saucepan of salted water to a boil. Cut each of the fennel bulbs into 6–8 wedges, depending on size. Then blanch them in the boiling water for 4 minutes, remove and add to a large bowl. Season well with salt and pepper, then add the nutmeg and sprinkle with chopped oregano, finely chopped garlic, and lemon rind. Pour over the cream and add the Parmesan, then mix well. Pour into an ovenproof dish and bake in the oven for 20 minutes.

To cook the skate: first ensure that the fish is dry before cooking by gently blotting it with paper towel. Heat the olive oil in a large skillet and fry the pieces of skate over a moderate heat, for 5 minutes on each side, finishing by pouring the butter over. Once cooked, pull the pan from the heat and pour the sauce over the skate. Bring back to a simmer for 1 minute, while you remove the gratin from the oven. Serve.

2 skate wings, about 12 ounces each, cut into 4 pieces

5 tablespoons olive oil

1 teaspoon melted butter

for the sauce

¼ pint (⅔ cup) olive oil

4 slices of bacon, cut into small pieces

4 anchovy fillets

1 tablespoon capers

a bunch of flat-leaf parsley, finely chopped

finely shredded rind and juice of 1 lemon

1 glass of white wine

9 fluid ounces (1 cup) tomato juice

salt and pepper

for the fennel gratin

4 fennel bulbs

a pinch of freshly shredded nutmeg

3 sprigs of oregano, chopped

1 garlic clove, finely chopped

finely shredded rind of 1 lemon

½ pint (1¼ cups) heavy cream

4 ounces (1⅜ cups) freshly shredded Parmesan cheese

gnocchi verdi
with sauce napoletana

First make the sauce: gently heat the oil in a saucepan, add the garlic and allow it to soften. While it does so, open your tomatoes and strain off the juice into a separate container; add the tomatoes to the garlic and oil. Bring the tomatoes to a boil and then turn down to the lowest heat and cook very gently for 30 minutes, pulping the tomatoes occasionally.

Make the gnocchi: if using fresh spinach ensure that you wash it thoroughly. You will probably need at least 4 standard bags – it cooks down to almost nothing. The best way to cook spinach is to heat a little oil or butter in a saucepan with a garlic clove and throw in the just-washed spinach leaves while still damp, stirring over a high heat for a couple of minutes. Tip the cooked spinach into a colander or strainer and allow it to cool naturally; nudging it around your colander will help to speed this up.

Once cooled, take small balls of spinach in your hand and squeeze tightly to try to remove as much water as possible. Then roughly chop the spinach. Sift the flour evenly across a large chopping board. Spread the chopped spinach evenly over the flour and season with salt, pepper, and nutmeg. Using a fork, start gently to work the spinach and flour together.

Strain any excess water from the ricotta, and again squeeze small handfuls of ricotta in your hands, to remove as much moisture as possible. Crumble the ricotta gently with your fingers into a large mixing bowl. Now add the spinach and seasoned flour mix, the Parmesan, and egg yolks. With a fork, gently and lightly work the ingredients together until they form a very rough dough.

Lightly flour a baking sheet that will fit in your refridgerator (or a couple of large plates will do). Take 2 teaspoons and scoop out a spoonful of dough with one, then gently press the second teaspoon face down over the first spoonful of dough and, with a flick of the wrist, scoop the mixture towards you with the second spoon, until your dough has swapped spoons. Repeat this three or four times and you have made a 'quenelle' (haute cuisine for dumpling). They should look like tiny eggs or airships. As each is made, place it carefully on the floured baking sheet, until you've used all the mixture. Now place the sheet in the refrigerator and allow your gnocchi to set for about an hour.

At this point, stir the reserved tomato liquid into your sauce and add the shredded basil leaves. Season and add the lemon juice. Pull the sauce from heat and bring a large saucepan of salted water to a boil. Add the gnocchi in three batches to the boiling water. When the gnocchi rises to the top of the water, remove them with a slotted spoon and gently dry by holding the base of the spoon on a dish towel. Start to plate up as the gnocchi are cooked, pouring over your tomato sauce and some shredded Parmesan cheese.

4 ounces cooked spinach

2 ounces (4 tablespoons) all-purpose flour, sifted, plus more for dusting

salt and pepper

a good pinch of freshly shredded nutmeg

9 ounces (1 cup) ricotta cheese

2 ounces (¾ cup) freshly shredded Parmesan cheese, plus more to serve

2 egg yolks

for the sauce napoletana

6 tablespoons olive oil

1 garlic clove, finely chopped

1 14 ounce can of tomatoes

bunch of basil leaves

juice of ½ lemon

Serves 6 as a starter or 4 as a main course

00 (doppio, or double, zero) flour is the Italian classification of flour graded suitable for pasta-making; it is now widely available in better supermarkets.

homemade ravioli of pumpkin

First make the pasta: put the flour and salt into a large bowl, make a well in the center and add 2 of the whole eggs and the extra yolks, with 2 tablespoons of the iced water. Slowly start to mix the dough with your fingertips, adding more iced water when necessary until it becomes a firm dough. Place it on a floured surface and knead for 2 minutes. Wrap in plastic wrap and chill.

To make the filling: preheat the oven to 400°F. Place the pumpkin wedges on a baking sheet, sprinkle with salt and pepper, brush with 4 tablespoons of the olive oil and scatter over the thyme. Cook in the oven for 40 minutes. Remove from the oven, leaving it on, and allow to cool.

Once cool, scrape the pumpkin flesh from the skin into a bowl, discarding the skin. Pour the pine nuts on to the baking sheet and quickly cook in the oven for about 2 minutes, just until golden. Remove and grind with a rolling pin. Then, with a fork, mash the ground pine nuts into the pumpkin pulp, adding the ricotta, grated Parmesan, mascarpone, 1 teaspoon of olive oil, egg yolk, lemon juice, and salt and pepper, mashing it all together well. Cover and chill for about 30 minutes.

Take one-quarter of the dough and roll it out into a long strip about 4 inches wide. Repeat with the rest of the dough.

Using a teaspoon, place blobs of filling along one side of the strips of pasta about ¾ inches apart. Brush around the edges of the pasta with a mixture of the remaining egg and a little milk, and fold the strips in half lengthwise over the filling. Push the edges down with your thumbs and cut into ravioli squares, making sure each is well sealed around the edges. Leave to rest.

Meanwhile, bring 2 pints (5 cups) of salted water to a boil and make the sauce: heat a large skillet and add to this the wine, broth, sage, lemon, and garlic. Bring to a boil and reduce by half. Slowly add the butter, whisking continuously. Once all the butter has been blended in, remove from the heat.

Add the ravioli to the boiling salted water and cook for 3 minutes, drain, then add to the sauce and warm gently over a low heat. Serve garnished with chives and a sprinkle of Parmesan.

for the pasta
14 ounces of 00 flour

a pinch of salt

3 whole eggs and 3 extra yolks

2–6 tablespoons iced water

a little milk, for sealing

for the filling
2 smallish pumpkins, each about 6 ounces, cut into wedges and seeds removed

salt and pepper

6 tablespoons olive oil

2 sprigs of fresh thyme, chopped

2 ounces (⅝ cup) pine nuts

9 ounces (1¼ cups) ricotta cheese

1¾ ounces (¾ cup) Parmesan cheese

5 ounces (1 cup) mascarpone cheese

1 egg yolk

juice of 1 lemon

for the sauce
½ glass of white wine

⅓ pint (¾ cup) vegetable broth

a sprig of sage

finely shredded rind of ½ lemon

½ garlic clove

2 ounces (½ stick) butter

to serve
a handful of chopped chives

shredded Parmesan cheese

Serves 6 as starter or 4 as main course

tagliarini with courgettes,
shrimp, mint, & parmesan

To make the pasta dough: place the flour in a mixing bowl, create a well in the center and add the whole eggs and egg yolks, the olive oil and a good pinch of salt. Mix to form a soft dough, adding a little iced water at this point if your dough is too hard. Turn the dough out on a floured work surface and continue kneading it until it is very smooth. Wrap the dough in plastic wrap and chill in refridgerator. Note: a very firm dough is preferable and must be worked by running it through the rollers of a pasta machine or by folding the pasta over on itself and repeating. This releases the glutens from the flour and gives it a very firm texture.

Feed the chilled dough through the pasta machine's cutters to make the tagliarini, dusting it with flour to ensure it doesn't stick to itself. If you don't have a pasta machine, flour the dough well, fold it over several times and cut across the folds into thin strips. Unfold the strips into tagliarini lengths.

Make the sauce: chop the onion, garlic, and celery as finely as possible; shred the zucchini. Drain the shrimp and pat them dry with a dish towel. Heat all the olive oil in a large skillet, add the shrimp and cook until browned. Add the mint, onions, garlic, celery and chile, and continue to cook until these are soft – the shrimp should now be a nutty brown. Add the cherry tomato halves and cook for a couple of minutes. Now stir in the lemon juice, then add the shredded zucchini and cook for a further 5 minutes. Add the white wine, cook for 2 minutes and pull the pan from heat.

Bring a large saucepan of salted water to a boil and cook the tagliarini for 2 minutes, drain through a strainer with a saucepan underneath to retain the cooking water. Bring this pan of water back to a boil and add a teaspoon of vegetable broth. Add the cooked tagliarini to the sauce, followed by two ladlefuls of the cooking water, the butter, and Parmesan. Using a wooden spoon, mix well over a moderate heat until glossy. Season and serve in a large bowl.

for the pasta

18 ounces of 00 (doppio zero) flour

6 eggs (you'll need 2 whole eggs and 4 yolks)

2 tablespoons of olive oil

a good pinch of salt

a little iced water (if required, to soften dough)

for the sauce

1 onion

2 garlic cloves

4 celery stalks

4 zucchini

1 pound peeled shrimp

8 tablespoons olive oil

a bunch of fresh mint, roughly chopped

1 red chile, seeded and finely chopped

a couple of handfuls of cherry tomatoes, halved

juice of 1 lemon

1 glass of white wine

to serve

¼ pint (⅔ cup) vegetable broth

2 ounces (½ stick) unsalted butter

4 ounces (1⅓ cups) freshly shredded Parmesan cheese

vegetable dishes

When cooked properly and dressed lightly with olive oil, vegetables are unbeatable. Here are just a few suggestions for vegetable dishes that can be served as a meal or as an accompaniment – and can be prepared easily in advance.

stuffed tomatoes
with mushrooms, parmesan, & spinach

I dedicate this recipe to my old vegetable chef, Juan, at Daphne's back in '92. All the young chefs thought the vegetable section meant just boiling beans and peas, but Juan proved them very wrong and made his section a real inspiration, with his wonderful creative ingredients.

8 large beef tomatoes

a handful of dried porcini mushrooms

4 tablespoons olive oil

2 packs of fresh spinach

8 flat-cap mushrooms

2 garlic cloves, chopped

2 sprigs of thyme, finely chopped

juice of 1 lemon

4 ounces (½ cup) cottage or ricotta cheese

2 ounces (¾ cup) freshly shredded Parmesan cheese

salt and pepper

a pinch of freshly grated nutmeg

1 egg yolk

1 red onion, chopped

1 red chile, seeded and chopped

for the dressing

½ teaspoon mustard

2 tablespoons white wine vinegar

6 tablespoons olive oil

4 basil leaves, cut into strips

First bring about 3 pints (7½ cups) of water to a boil and blanch the tomatoes for 1 minute. Remove with a slotted spoon and place in a bowl of iced water (this makes the skins peel away from the flesh easily). Put to one side. Now add the porcini mushrooms to the still-boiling water and pull the saucepan off the heat. Leave the mushrooms to soak.

Heat the olive oil in a large skillet and add the chilli, onions and garlic and cook on a moderate heat until soft. Set aside. Cook the spinach on a moderate heat for 2 minutes and then pour through a strainer with a bowl beneath. Using a wooden spoon, press it firmly against the strainer so any liquid drips into the bowl. Tip the spinach onto a chopping board and place to one side. Slice the flat-cap mushrooms lengthwise, then widthwise into rough cubes. Place to one side. Using a slotted spoon, gently remove the porcini mushrooms from the hot water and finely chop them. Add the spinach water to the mushroom water to give you a vegetable broth. Strain the broth through a strainer.

Place the pan back on the heat with a good dash of olive oil and fry the porcini and fresh mushrooms over a high heat for 3–4 minutes until colored. Turn the heat down to moderate and pour over ½ pint (1¼ cups) of the broth. Add the garlic, thyme, and the lemon juice. Continue to cook the mushrooms until all the liquid has been cooked out and the mushrooms are shiny. Remove from heat and allow to cool.

Strain the cottage cheese through a strainer and gently push it against the strainer to remove as much liquid as possible. Finely chop the spinach and put it in a bowl. Stir in the mushrooms, cottage cheese, two-thirds of the Parmesan, salt, pepper, and nutmeg. Chill.

Preheat the oven to 325°F. Peel the tomatoes and cut the tops off, about a third of the way down, reserving them to replace as lids. Using a teaspoon, carefully scoop out the pulp of the tomatoes, reserving it for the dressing. Take the spinach and mushroom mix from the fridge and fold the egg yolk into it. Using the teaspoon again, stuff the tomatoes with the mix. Don't press the mixture down or the tomatoes may split, but over-fill the tomatoes so the mix is bursting out over the tops. Sprinkle the rest of the Parmesan on top and put the tomato tops back on, tilted at a jaunty angle. Carefully place the tomatoes in an oven dish and drizzle with olive oil, place in the oven and cook for 20–30 minutes.

Meanwhile, make the dressing: combine the reserved tomato juice and pulp with the oil, mustard, vinegar, and basil. Whisk together and pour over the cooked tomatoes.

Try to get the orange-fleshed sweet potatoes as they are better-flavored and richer in nutrients.

You could use other winter squashes in place of pumpkin. Many, like the tasty butternut and acorn squashes, are now becoming much more widely available.

pumpkin gratin

Some of my favorite vegetable dishes I discovered on my travels in Australia. There, due to the climate, they have a very large variety of Mediterranean and northern European vegetables, and the Australians' no-holds-barred attitude to cooking them was always inventive and inspiring. Unlike European cooking, which tends to be far more structured, it was sometimes a rather hit-or-miss affair. Here's one of the hits.

2 pounds pumpkin

5 tablespoons olive oil

2 large sweet potatoes

1 pound peas (preferably fresh but frozen are fine)

6 sprigs of thyme

finely shredded rind of 1 lemon and juice of ½

1 garlic clove, finely chopped

1 chile, seeded and finely chopped

½ glass of white wine

1 pint (2½ cups) vegetable broth

salt and pepper

1 ounce (6 tablespoons) freshly shredded Parmesan cheese

1¾ oz. (3½ tablespoons) breadcrumbs

Preheat the oven to 350°F. Carefully cut the pumpkin into 8 wedges, leaving the skin on. Using a dessertspoon, remove the seeds from the wedges. Pour 1 tablespoon of olive oil on to a baking sheet, place the wedges on it and roast for 20 minutes. This slightly dehydrates the pumpkin, intensifying the taste; it also softens the flesh, making it easier to remove from the skin.

Peel the sweet potatoes and cut them into discs about ¾ inch thick. Put them in a large mixing bowl and set to one side. If using fresh peas, add them to the sweet potatoes; if using frozen, wait and add the peas for the last 10 minutes of cooking. Remove the thyme leaves from the stalks and chop the leaves. Add this with the lemon juice, garlic, and chile to the sweet potatoes (and peas) and mix well.

The pumpkin should now be ready. Remove from the oven and, using a knife, remove the flesh from the skin and cut the flesh into rough cubes. Mix the pumpkin cubes in with the sweet potatoes (and peas). Now pour over the wine and the vegetable broth, and season with salt and pepper. Place in a 16 inch ovenproof dish, cover with aluminum foil and make a small hole in the center of the foil to let the steam out. Cook in the oven for 20 minutes.

While this is cooking, mix together the Parmesan, breadcrumbs, and lemon rind. After 20 minutes, remove the foil from the dish (stir in frozen peas now), sprinkle the breadcrumb mix over the top and cook for a further 10 minutes until nicely browned on top.

green bean
& broccoli gratin

The advantage of cooking vegetables in this way is that you retain all their goodness as opposed to boiling where a lot of that goodness is thrown away in the cooking water. This dish is wonderful with fresh fish.

Preheat the oven to 350°F. Cut the broccoli lengthwise into long stems, retaining the stalks. Gently heat the olive oil in a large skillet with the chopped garlic. Add the broccoli and seal it in the hot oil for 5 minutes over a moderate heat. Pour over the vegetable broth and bring to a boil, then remove the pan from the heat.

   Add the cannellini beans, parsley, tarragon, a good twist of fresh black pepper and a pinch of salt. Pour the contents of the pan into an ovenproof dish, cover with aluminum foil and cook for 10 minutes.

2 heads of broccoli, about 1 pound

4 tablespoons olive oil

2 garlic cloves, finely chopped

⅔ pint (1¾ cups) vegetable broth

1 14 ounce can of cannellini beans, drained and rinsed

a handful of flat-leaf parsley, finely chopped

a sprig of tarragon, finely chopped

salt and pepper

honey-roast cabbage

salt

1 large green cabbage

1 teaspoon English mustard

2 tablespoons honey

1 inch piece of fresh ginger, shredded

1 Spanish onion, thinly sliced

a bunch of parsley (either type), chopped

4 slices of smoked back bacon (optional), finely chopped

juice of ½ lemon

Preheat the oven to 275°F and bring a large saucepan of salted water to a boil. Cut the cabbage across two-thirds of the way through and again at right angles, taking care not to cut all the way through to the other side, so you have cut a cross shape into the crown of the cabbage. Put the cabbage in the boiling water, stalk end up, and cook for 6 minutes. Remove the cabbage and allow to drain. Keep ¼ pint (⅝ cup) of the cabbage water in the pan and discard the rest. Add the mustard, honey, ginger, onion, parsley, bacon, and lemon juice to the pan and simmer gently for 3 minutes.

   Lay out a large sheet of aluminum foil and place the cabbage in the center, then pull the edges of the foil up around the cabbage to form a nest. Spoon over all the sauce you have just made. Bring the edges of the foil together around the cabbage, place in the oven and cook for 1 hour.

   Remove and serve, the scores you made in the cabbage initially will now fall open to give you 4 perfect portions as you unwrap the foil.

Don't refresh the
potatoes when you
drain them as the
warm potatoes will
absorb all the flavors
of the dressing.

new potatoes
with tomato, cucumber, olive,
and rosemary dressing

1 pound new potatoes
finely shredded rind
of 1 lemon, to serve

for the dressing
4 beef tomatoes
2 garlic cloves
5 tablespoons olive oil
1 sprig of rosemary
4 anchovy fillets
½ teaspoon green
peppercorns (canned
or jarred)
a pinch of sugar
a handful of pitted
olives
2 tablespoons red
wine vinegar
½ cucumber

This makes a great accompaniment to broiled chicken, pork, or boned fish.

Prepare the dressing: bring 2 pints (5 cups) of water to a boil. Score the tops of
the tomatoes with a cross shape and, with a small knife, remove the stalk of the
tomatoes. Place the garlic cloves and the tomatoes in the boiling water for about
12 seconds, remove with a slotted spoon and leave to dry. Pull the saucepan to
one side, saving the water to cook the potatoes.

Pour all the olive oil into another saucepan off the heat. Peel the tomatoes
and chop them until you have a tomato pulp. Crush the garlic with the side of a
knife. Strip the rosemary from the stalk and finely chop. Add to the olive oil.
Slice the anchovy fillets lengthwise and add them, together with the strained
green peppercorns.

Place the oil over a low heat and gently cook for about 3 minutes, stirring
occasionally. Add the chopped tomatoes with a pinch of sugar and gently bring to
a boil, then simmer for 5 minutes. While this is simmering, roughly chop the
olives and add them to the tomatoes, together with the red wine vinegar, and pull
from heat immediately.

Bring the first saucepan back to a boil and slice the new potatoes lengthwise,
about 1¼–1½ inches thick. Add these to the saucepan and boil for 12–15
minutes until just tender. Drain well and put in a large mixing bowl, pour over the
warm tomato dressing and mix well. Finely chop the cucumber, add and mix
again. Pour into a large flat dish and serve sprinkled with lemon rind.

braised broccoli,
peas, & jerusalem artichoke, mint, & chile

1 pound Jerusalem artichokes

2 heads of broccoli

2 garlic cloves, finely chopped

1 red chile, seeded and finely chopped

a bunch of mint, chopped

1 teaspoon red wine vinegar

a good pinch of salt

1 pint (2½ cups) vegetable broth

1 carrot

1 glass of white wine

8 ounces fresh peas (if available, but frozen will do)

2 tablespoons olive oil

Preheat the oven to 325°F. Peel the artichokes; trim the broccoli and cut lengthwise, stalks and all, into long pieces. Put the garlic, chile, and mint into a bowl, spoon over the vinegar, add a good pinch of salt and put to one side, allowing the juices of the chile and mint to be drawn out by the salt and vinegar.

Put the vegetable broth in a large saucepan and bring to a boil. Meanwhile, slice the carrot into discs. Add the carrots to the boiling broth and boil for 4 minutes exactly, then add the artichokes and pull from the heat. Add the wine and peas off the heat.

Pour the chile-mint marinade and the oil into a large deep baking dish, place the broccoli over it and then pour over the contents of the saucepan. Cover with aluminum foil, prick the foil with a fork, place in oven and cook for 20 minutes.

roast root vegetables

This dish requires a little bit of time and a lot of olive oil, but can be served with just about anything, and you can vary the vegetables with the season.

2 sweet potatoes

8 ounces turnips

2 parsnips

8 ounces carrots

1 small head of celery root

1 potato

1 whole head of garlic

4 sprigs of thyme

salt

9 fluid ounces (1 cup) olive oil

Preheat the oven to 350°F and a large roasting pan. Peel all the root vegetables, then cut the sweet potatoes into 1½ inch discs, the turnips into halves, the parsnips and carrots into sixths, the celery root into good-sized wedges, the potato into eighths. Break the garlic into individual cloves, discarding any loose skin, but do not peel. Strip the thyme leaves from the stalks, discard the stalks and chop the leaves finely, then place them to one side.

Bring large saucepan of water to a boil and blanch all the root vegetables and garlic for 3–4 minutes. Drain and allow to cool. Tip the root vegetables out onto paper towel and gently rub until completely dry. Sprinkle them with a good pinch of salt.

Put all the vegetable into a large mixing bowl and pour over the olive oil, add the finely chopped thyme leaves and mix well. Carefully remove the roasting pan from the oven and pour all of the vegetables and olive oil evenly over the pan. Place back in the oven and roast for 35 minutes, reducing the oven setting to 325° for the final 10 minutes.

portuguese lentils

9 ounces (1½ cups)
Puy lentils

1 bay leaf

6 tomatoes

1 red chile

2 garlic cloves,
finely chopped

½ cucumber, peeled
and finely chopped

2 red onions, finely
chopped

for the dressing

2 tablespoons white
wine vinegar

6 tablespoons
olive oil

a bunch of basil leaves

½ teaspoon celery salt

pepper

The use of pulses has become a lot more commonplace again lately. Although once laughed at as a hippie substitute for meat, two-thirds of the world's population are reliant on pulses for their main source of protein. This particular dish is popular across southern Europe. I discovered it while on holiday in Portugal with my old friend Eddie De Vihena, who is never happier than when he's back home in the Algarve, eating *lentilhas a portuguesas*. Here's how to make them.

Cut the tomatoes into quarters, scoop out the seeds and juice, put these in a bowl and place to one side; chop the tomato flesh into cubes. Cut the red chile in half lengthwise, remove and discard the seeds and chop the chile finely. Add the chile and garlic to the tomato seeds and pulp (the acid in the tomato actually slightly cooks the garlic and chile, giving them a slightly soft and mellower taste). Put the cubed tomato flesh, cucumber, and onions in a large mixing bowl.

Put the lentils, bay leaf, and 3 pints (7½ cups) of water in a saucepan and bring to a boil. Allow to simmer for no longer than 20 minutes (any longer than this and you are moving into dhal territory). Drain the lentils and add immediately to the tomato and cucumber. Toss to mix well.

Make the dressing: add the vinegar and olive oil to the tomato seeds and pulp, chile, and garlic. Using a whisk, beat thoroughly and finish by adding the shredded basil leaves. Season with celery salt and freshly ground pepper. Pour the dressing over the lentils while still hot, so the lentils absorb the dressing. Eat.

desserts

What is a dinner party without a dessert – or two? Nothing sets the scene better when you go to the table than a glistening fruit tart or chocolate cake sitting on the sideboard. It is always a good idea, if you can, to choose a dessert that you can make in advance, so you can relax yourself through the later stages of the meal.

pavlova
with frozen raspberry yogurt

First make the frozen raspberry yogurt: put the raspberries in a large saucepan with the sugar and vanilla essence, 2 tablespoons of water, and 1 teaspoon of lemon juice. Gently bring to a boil, purée and allow to cool.

Fill another saucepan one-third full of water and bring to a boil, then reduce to simmer. Put the egg yolks and a teaspoon of water in a large heatproof bowl and place over the saucepan. Whisk the egg yolks until pale and fluffy, the consistency of shaving foam. Remove from the heat and continue to whisk for another 30 seconds or so to ensure the yolk mix does not stick to the heated bowl. Fold two-thirds of the now-cooled raspberry purée into the egg yolk mix and add the yogurt. Fold together and place in an ice-cream machine for 40–60 minutes.

For most of us who don't have an ice-cream machine, pour the mixture into a plastic bag, tie a knot in the top and chuck it in the freezer for 10 minutes. Remove the bag, give it a shake (don't squeeze it with your hands, as this warms the cooling mixture up again), put it back in the freezer and keep repeating this process every 10 minutes for the next hour. After all this, for the first time your homemade ice cream – or, in this case, frozen yogurt – will be so delicious that it is likely you will run out and buy yourself an ice-cream maker, because of the labor-intensive process of making it by hand!

Make the pavlova: turn your oven on at the lowest possible setting. Bring another saucepan half-filled with water to a boil and again place a clean mixing bowl over it. After 2 minutes, remove the warmed bowl and pour the egg whites into it. Immediately start to whisk vigorously, adding the sugar slowly, a tablespoon at a time, into the fluffing egg whites. Continue whisking until the egg whites are firm and peaking with a glossy sheen.

Place a sheet of waxed paper on each of 2 baking sheets, then lightly brush them with oil. Put serving-spoon dollops of the meringue mixture on to the prepared sheets, leaving at least 3 inches between each. You should have about 12 in all, preferably 6 on each sheet. Place in the oven and cook for at least 1 hour 40 minutes, keeping the oven on the lowest possible setting. As ovens vary on their lowest setting, cooking time could be anything up to 2 hours.

Once the meringues are cooked (when tapped gently they sound hollow), remove from the oven and allow to cool. When they are cool, use a bread knife to cut each meringue in half like a roll. Take curled scoops of your iced yogurt by dragging a dessertspoon over the yogurt's surface, place one in the middle of each meringue base, pop the top back on and press down gently. Once all of the meringues are stuffed, pour the remaining raspberry purée over their tops and serve on a large dish.

When making meringue, ensure all your equipment is spotlessly clean and grease-free. This will help the egg whites to get volume and ensure that your meringue mix will become stiff.

If you can get an ice-cream machine, then do – homemade ice-creams and sorbets are so delicious. The good machines last forever and cover anything from savory sorbets to cookie-infused ice-creams. If you have children, they love making and, of course, eating the stuff. You can also be sure that the ice-cream you are making is free from animal fats and additives.

whites of 6 eggs

12 ounces (1¾ cups) superfine sugar

vegetable oil, for brushing

for the frozen raspberry yogurt

1 pound of raspberries

2 ounces (4 tablespoons) superfine sugar

2 drops of vanilla extract

1 teaspoon lemon juice

2 egg yolks

18 fluid ounces (2 cups) plain runny yogurt

goat cheese & pear crostata
with chile lime syrup

Fruit served with cheese at the end of a meal is a culinary tradition, the two complementing each other so well. This recipe combines the flavors of the fruit and cheese, and is a wonderful alternative to cheesecake.

Preheat the oven to 350°F. Roll out the puff pastry to a rectangle slightly larger than a sheet of A4 paper. Place it on a chopping board and put it in the refridgerator to allow it to rest before cooking.

Peel the apples and pears and core them, then cut them into thin slices. Place the sliced fruit in a large bowl and pour over the juice of 1 of the limes. Using a hot wet knife, cut the goat cheese in half lengthwise, and slice these across into the thinnest half moons of cheese you can manage.

Remove the pastry from the refridgerator. In a small bowl, whisk the egg with a touch of milk and brush this glaze around the edges of the pastry, about ½ inch in all the way round. Now place a slice of apple followed by one of pear across the pastry in lines, ensuring you leave the same gap of clear pastry around the edge. Arrange the goat cheese slices to overlap between the lines of fruit as evenly as you can. I'm suggesting you do it this way as I often find that there are always many more slices of fruit than goat cheese, unless you've sliced it incredibly thinly.

Place the crostata in the oven and cook for 15–20 minutes, until crisp around the edges and the fruit is golden brown – the cheese should have slightly melted and have a dark-brown crispy surface. Remove from oven and allow to rest for 5 minutes.

Whilst the crostata is cooking and resting, make the chile lime syrup: using a pestle and mortar, grind the chile to a paste with the sugar. Add the lime juice, followed by the olive oil, a small pinch of salt, and a twist of black pepper. Mix together well. If you don't have a pestle and mortar, use the back of a spoon in a bowl. Gently drizzle this over the crostata.

14 ounces puff pastry

2 cooking apples

2 pears

juice of 1 lime

8 ounces goat cheese log

1 egg

a splash of milk

for the chile lime syrup

1 red chile, seeded and chopped

1 tablespoon granulated sugar

juice of 1 lime

2 tablespoons olive oil

salt and pepper

Serves 4–6

tiramisu

This is a recipe from my days at Armani Express. It was a good deal for a young chef, as they'd dress me – which I needed. Unfortunately my waistline has thickened a little since then.

Separate the egg yolks and whites into 2 bowls. Vigorously whisk the yolks, slowly adding 2½ tablespoons of sugar, until pale and frothy. Now vigorously whisk the whites, slowly adding the rest of the sugar, until standing in stiff peaks. Add the mascarpone and vanilla extract to the egg yolks and fold in gently. Now pour in the egg whites and again fold them in gently. Wipe the empty bowl clean, add the heavy cream and whisk until just thickened. Fold this gently into the egg mixture.

Now use the beans to make strong black coffee in a cafetière or simply pour the boiling water over the coffee in a heatproof bowl and strain it after a few minutes. Pour the coffee into a mixing bowl and add the Marsala and brandy. Stir and allow to cool.

In a large deep dish about 12 x 8 inches and about 4 inches deep, spread a 2 inch thick layer of mascarpone mixture over the base. Take the sponge fingers one by one and quickly dip them into the cooled coffee mixture for only 1 second per finger and place over the mascarpone mixture in rows. Continue until you have a layer of biscuits, then pour over another 1 inch thick layer of mascarpone mix. Repeat the layers, finishing with the mascarpone mix. Finely shred the dark plain chocolate over the top and chill in refridgerator for at least 3–4 hours. Eat.

The word tiramisu is from the Italian for 'pick-me-up'. This is probably because of the kick given by the dessert's coffee and alcohol content.

Everyone seems to think of tiramisu as an old Italian classic but it is, in fact, a relatively recent dish that is quite probably more popular outside of Italy than it is in its country of origin – apart from in the many restaurants that cater for tourists. Little Italian savoiardi are the sponge fingers of choice.

4 eggs

4 tablespoons superfine sugar

18 ounces mascarpone cheese

2 drops of vanilla extract

5 fluid ounces (½ cup) heavy cream

4 tablespoons freshly ground coffee (the mocha used for espresso is best, or a good instant will do)

10 fluid ounces (1¼ cups) boiling water

4 tablespoons Marsala

2 tablespoons brandy

2 packets of sponge fingers

9 ounces dark plain chocolate

key lime pie
with peppered strawberries & amaretto crème fraîche

I've tried a few versions of this dish in my time, but this particular recipe is my favorite. It's also a great alternative to lemon tart, of which I am also very fond.

Preheat the oven to 300°F. Roll out the pastry, sprinkling it with the rind of 2 of the limes, and use to line a 10 inch tart pan. First we need to bake the pastry shell blind or it won't cook completely in the time it takes to cook the filling. Pierce the base of the pastry several times with a fork, line with waxed paper or aluminum foil, pour baking beans or rice over that to come halfway up the sides. Bake for 20 minutes. Remove from the oven and allow to sit for 5 minutes before removing the baking beans and lining paper. Place the tart shell to one side to cool.

In a large mixing bowl, mix together well the lime juice and remaining rind, the condensed milk, egg yolks, softened butter, and heavy cream. Pour this mixture into the tart shell, place in the oven and cook for about 30–40 minutes until nicely set.

While this is cooking, make the Amaretto crème fraîche: pour the amaretto into a saucepan, slowly bring to a boil and pull from heat. Spoon the crème fraîche into a bowl and pour in the Amaretto, mix well with the sugar and place this Amaretto cream in the refridgerator until needed.

Take your pie out of the oven, allow to cool and then place in the refrigerator to chill. Remove the stalks from the strawberries and place in a bowl with several good twists of black pepper, a pinch of sugar, and a squeeze of lime. Mix together gently but well.

When you are ready to serve, pour the strawberries over the top of the key lime pie and serve each slice with a dollop of Amaretto crème fraîche.

Chefs call the paper lining of a pastry shell a 'cartouche' and there is a clever way of making one. Take a piece of waxed paper or aluminum foil about A3 size and fold it over in half widthwise, then in half again left to right, then roll into a cone, taking the bottom left-hand corner and roll it up to the top right edge. Place this over the tart shell with the point of the cone in the center of the tart shell and tear away any excess paper or foil over the outer edge of the tart shell. Now unfold the cone and you should have a disc of paper which fits neatly inside the tart shell over the pastry.

9 ounces of sweet pastry

juice of 10 limes and the finely shredded rind of 5

14 fluid ounces (1¾ cups) condensed milk

5 egg yolks

2 ounces (½ stick) unsalted butter, softened

4 tablespoons heavy cream

8 ounces strawberries

pepper

a pinch of sugar

a squeeze of lime juice

for the amaretto crème fraîche

3 tablespoons Amaretto

7 fluid ounces (¾ cup) crème fraîche

1 teaspoon granulated sugar

panettone & brioche butter pudding

Preheat the oven to 275°F and a moderate broiler. Slice the pannetone and brioche as you would bread, then gently broil on both sides, keeping a close eye on them as you do, as they broil quickly and it's pretty depressing to burn the whole lot. Place the toasted slices on a chopping board.

Gently melt the butter in a small skillet, lightly brush the sides and base of a medium-sized ovenproof dish with the melted butter. Lay the brioche and pannetone slices in layers in the dish, overlapping the slices.

In a heatproof bowl, add the superfine sugar to the egg yolks. Gently heat the milk and cream together in a saucepan until hot but not simmering. Slowly pour half the milk and cream mixture over the egg yolks while whisking, then add the whisked egg yolks, milk, and cream back to the saucepan, together with the remaining cream and milk. Place the saucepan back on the heat, add the split vanilla pods or extract, stir until simmering and then strain over the pannetone and brioche. Sprinkle with Demerara sugar and cook in the oven for 30 minutes.

Once cooked, this dish can be served immediately or can easily be reheated in the oven or microwaved. It goes very well with vanilla ice-cream or just with plain cream poured over the top.

1 medium-sized fruit pannetone

1 small brioche loaf

3 ounces (6 tablespoons) unsalted butter

3 ounces (½ cup) superfine sugar

3 egg yolks

1 pint (2½ cups) milk

½ pint (1¼ cups) heavy cream

2 vanilla pods or 3 drops of vanilla extract

1 tablespoon Demerara sugar

vanilla ice-cream or cream, to serve

chocolate ricotta tart

If you have the time, make the pastry yourself. Known as pasta frolla, it is more crumbly and melt-in-the-mouth than ordinary sweet pastry, so it is really worth it. Otherwise just use a packet of sweet pastry. If you like, you can decorate the tart with curls of ganache as on page 168.

First make the pastry: preheat the oven to 350°F. Add the flour, salt, and butter to a large mixing bowl and rub through with your fingers until they have the consistency of breadcrumbs. Mix in the egg, together with 3 tablespoons cold water and the sugar. Knead the mixture lightly and gently to ensure a light crumbly pastry. Form the pastry into a ball, wrap gently in plastic wrap and chill in the refridgerator for 30 minutes.

While the pastry is resting, make the filling: place the ricotta in a strainer to drain off any excess water. Once it has drained, put it in a mixing bowl and gradually beat in the sugar and the eggs with a spoon. Stir in the citrus rind and juice. Now add the almonds and the chopped mixed peel, the vanilla extract and the shredded chocolate, mixing well between each addition. Chill this mix in the refrigerator.

Remove the pastry while you're in there, roll it out on a well floured surface and use it to line a 10 inch tart pan. Cut away any excess pastry, keeping it for a lattice top if you would prefer it to the curls of ganache. Pour the ricotta mix into the tart and smooth over evenly. If using the pastry trimmings, roll them out and cut into 1 inch width strips. Arrange these in a lattice pattern over the top of the tart. Bake in the oven for 45–50 minutes, until a light golden brown. Remove the tart from the oven and allow to cool. Dust with confectioners' sugar when cool.

12 ounces (1½ cups) ricotta cheese

3 ounces (¼ cup) superfine sugar

3 eggs

finely shredded rind and juice of 1 lemon

finely shredded rind and juice of ½ orange

2 ounces (⅓ cup) blanched almonds, finely chopped

2 ounces (½ cup) chopped mixed peel

4 drops of vanilla extract

4 ounces dark plain chocolate, shredded

confectioners' sugar, to dust

for the pasta frolla

8 ounces (2 cups) all-purpose flour, plus more for dusting

a pinch of salt

4 ounces (1 stick) unsalted butter

1 egg

1 ounce (2 tablespoons) superfine sugar

amaretto brûlée

All over Europe there are different names for roughly this dish – custard with a glazed sugar topping. I am of the opinion that the person who invented this dish got around a bit or it's just the simplest dessert to make.

Preheat the oven to 230°F and bring a large saucepanful of water to a boil. Place the egg yolks and sugar in a mixing bowl. Heat the milk, split vanilla pod or extract and the cream gently. Once the mixture comes to a boil, remove from the heat and pour the contents of the pan into the mixing bowl, stirring continuously. Continue stirring until the mixture has cooled a little, then pour all the mixture into a jug.

Place six 3 inch ramekins in a deep oven dish and carefully pour the custard mixture into each ramekin to as close to the rim as possible. Place the oven tray on the lowest shelf of your oven, pull the shelf out halfway and carefully fill the oven dish half-full with the boiling water. Push the shelf slowly back into the oven and cook for 30–40 minutes, until firm.

Carefully remove each ramekin from the water. Turn the oven off and allow the water in the oven tray to cool before removing the tray from the oven. Once the ramekins have cooled slightly, chill them in the refridgerator for at least 30 minutes.

To make the topping: pour the amaretto and sugar into a saucepan and gently bring to a boil, stirring occasionally. Reduce the liquid by two-thirds, until thick and bubbling and dark caramel in color – this is known by confectioners as 'toffee stage.' Gently spoon this mixture over the cooled custards and allow the sugar to set, about 3 minutes. Add the topping just before serving, as the sugar will only stay crisp for a short while before becoming soft like caramel.

You can, of course, make a whole family of brûlées using different liqueurs – among the best are Grand Marnier, cherry brandy, Tia Maria and crème de cassis.

Mixing some fruit into the syrup for the topping also gives delicious results – try raspberries, sliced strawberries, blueberries, or sliced ripe apricots, peaches or nectarines.

4 large egg yolks

2 ounces (¼ cup) granulated sugar

¼ pint (⅔ cup) milk

1 vanilla pod, split, or 2 drops of vanilla extract

10 fluid ounces (1¼ cups) heavy cream

for the topping

2 tablespoons Amaretto

8 tablespoons superfine sugar

Serves 6

chocolate truffle cake
with ganache

For a truly sensational taste, you need to use good-quality plain, dark, semi-sweet chocolate. For this recipe I have used Grand Marnier, but you can use brandy if you prefer.

Preheat the oven to 350°F and grease two 10 inch cake pans with butter, then line the bases with baking paper and dust with flour.

Bring to a boil a large saucepan one-third filled with water, and reduce to simmer. Break the chocolate into a heatproof mixing bowl that will sit in the pan without touching the water and place over the simmering water. Once the chocolate has melted, pull the pan from the heat.

In a separate bowl, whisk together the egg yolks and half the sugar until frothy. Add the butter to the melted chocolate and stir until that has melted, then stir in the milk, followed by the Grand Marnier. Pull from the heat and stir in the egg yolk mixture, followed by the ground almonds.

In a third mixing bowl, whisk the egg whites with a pinch of salt until standing in stiff peaks, then fold in the remaining sugar. Slowly fold the egg whites into the chocolate mixture and stir gently until blended. Pour the mixture into the prepared pans, smooth the surfaces evenly and bake in the oven for 10–15 minutes, until a knife inserted into the center comes out clean.

Remove from the oven, leave to cool in the pans for 15 minutes and then turn out on a cooling rack to cool completely. When the cakes are quite cool, melt the apricot jam in a saucepan with a little water, and brush this mix over the sides and top of the cake.

Make the filling: melt the chocolate as above, stir in the milk and pull from the heat. Whisk in the egg yolk. Whisk the egg white until standing in soft peaks and fold in the sugar. Now gently stir the chocolate and egg whites together to form a mousse-like filling. Spread the filling over the bottom half of the cake, place the other on top and put the whole thing in the refridgerator to set.

Make the ganache: melt the chocolate as above, stir in the butter, pull from the heat and allow to cool. Whip the heavy cream to stiff peaks, add the Grand Marnier and fold this into the cooled chocolate mixture.

Place the cake back on the cooling rack and sit the rack on a large dish or tray. Slowly pour the ganache over the cake, ensuring you cover the top and sides. Place the cake back in the refridgerator to set again. This cake will keep for up to 2 days.

4½ ounces (9 tablespoons) unsalted butter, plus more for greasing

flour, for dusting

7 ounces plain dark chocolate

4 eggs, separated

4½ ounces (⅔ cup) superfine sugar

2 tablespoons milk

1 tablespoon Grand Marnier

4½ ounces (1¼ cups) ground almonds

a pinch of salt

2 tablespoons apricot jam, for glazing

for the filling

2½ ounces plain dark chocolate

2 tablespoons milk

1 egg, separated

½ ounce (1 tablespoon) superfine sugar

for the ganache

9 ounces plain dark chocolate

2 ounces (½ stick) unsalted butter

9 fluid ounces heavy cream

1 tablespoon Grand Marnier

A couple of summers back, I spent a wonderful few weeks with my old friend Eddie de Vihena in Portugal...evenings by the pool, cooking just-caught fish on the barbecue....When we got back to London, Eddie, the old romantic, decided to try to reproduce some traditional Portuguese barbecue dishes for his girlfriend in their flat in Fulham. He nipped out and bought a disposable barbecue from the local service station, placed it on the stove and proceeded happily to cook chicken piri piri. Very involved in his cooking, he failed to notice the amount of smoke pouring out of his house. A vigilant neighbor assumed the house was on fire and, sure enough, firemen were soon pounding at his front door. His flat smells of charred chicken to this day.

I have assembled as many recipes from my travels as from back home, so this is a fairly eclectic chapter. Most of these dishes will be cooked over open coals. Do not despair if you don't have a garden, or even a balcony, these dishes can easily be served indoors if cooked on a griddle pan.

barbecues

grilled marinated squid

This is a wonderfully simple dish and, yet again, careful preparation is essential to ensure great results.

Remove the wings and outer skin of the squid under gently running water. Cut away the tentacles just below the eyes and squeeze out the small beak you'll find at the center of the tentacles. Place the tentacles in a colander. Using the knife, make a lengthwise slit along one side of each squid so you can open up the tube. Scrape out and discard the guts and cartilage. Using a serrated steak knife, score incisions in a cross-hatch across the inside of the squid from left to right, and then repeat the other way to help tenderize the squid. Carefully pat dry.

Make the marinade: put the chiles and garlic in a mixing bowl. Add the olive oil and a pinch of salt. Place the dry squid tubes into this marinade, mix well and place to one side to marinate for at least 30 minutes, preferably longer.

Make the dressing: remove all the leaves from the oregano and grind them using a pestle and mortar if you have one; if not, finely chop the leaves. Mix the oregano with a good pinch of salt and grind into a paste. Squeeze in the lemon juice and mix well. Now add the olive oil and mix well with a good twist of black pepper to finish.

Remove the squid from the marinade and cook on the preheated hot barbecue, scored side down first. As the squid cooks, it slowly rolls into a tube and the natural juices of the squid will caramelize on one side. Then turn the squid over after about 3–4 minutes and cook on the other side; the squid should not be at all pink inside once it is cooked.

Toss in the dressing to serve. This dish works wonderfully well with Portuguese Lentils (page 85).

In Italy, this type of fresh herb dressing is known as *salmoriglio*.

Note for the squeamish thinking about gutting the sardines opposite – salt water fish tend not to have much innards.

8 fresh squid, each about 3 ounces, or an 8 ounce bag of frozen squid tubes, defrosted

for the marinade
2 red chiles, seeded and finely chopped
2 garlic cloves, finely chopped
3 tablespoons olive oil
a good pinch of salt

for the dressing
a bunch of fresh oregano
juice of 1 lemon
5 tablespoons olive oil
pepper

dressed sardines

Young chefs tend to move around an awful lot, gleaning as much knowledge from their head chefs as possible. This recipe was pinched, I have to admit, from possibly two of the most influential chefs I've worked for, Rosie and Ruth at the River Café in London– and I hope my hard work helped them at least a little bit on their way to success, as much as their training has helped me.

First prepare the dressing: in a bowl, mix the mint, vinegar, celery salt, chopped shallots, lemon rind and chiles. Place to one side.

Run a sharp knife along the underside (belly) of the sardine. Under very gentle running water, using the best kitchen tool of all, the index finger, remove the fish's innards. At this point, still under running water, gently scrape off any outer scales from the fish, ensuring you remove all of them – they come away easily using your thumb or a table knife. Using a dish towel, dry the sardines well to help avoid their sticking to the broiler.

Pour the flour on to one large plate and drizzle a little olive oil on another. Dip the sardines into the flour on both sides to coat, and then lightly pull the fish through the olive oil. Place on the preheated hot barbecue and cook the for about 5 minutes on each side.

Finish the dressing by adding the oil and seasoning with salt and pepper. Lay the cooked sardines on a large plate and spoon over the delicious fresh, tangy dressing – the perfect accompaniment for sardines.

12 fresh (as fresh as possible) sardines

1 ounce (2 tablespoons) all-purpose flour

a little olive oil, for coating

for the dressing

a large bunch of mint, finely shredded

2 tablespoons red wine vinegar

a pinch of celery salt

2 shallots, finely chopped

shredded rind of 2 lemons

pinch of dried chiles

2 tablespoons olive oil

salt and pepper

dave's lindian tuna

I've been going to Lindos on the island of Rhodes for quite a few years now. At one time, a good friend of mine, Dave, had a club there called 'Jodie's Flat'. Dave and the boys are still regulars on Lindos, and he has introduced me to many of the locals and, naturally, local food. Although there may be a few too many tourists there these days, one thing's for sure...there could never be too many fish. Another regular on Lindos, Claudio, an Italian blessed with quite exceptional fishing skills, would often invite us out on his speedboat to catch tuna. My attitude towards these excursions was that they were relaxing days out, fishing on the Aegean, whereas to Claudio it was a hunting expedition and anything less than a catch of five fish was nothing short of a disgrace.

A regular fishing trip usually started in this way: 'Eduardo, Eduardo, come, come we go feeshing.' We'd all pile on the boat and blast out to sea, Claudio, of course, at the wheel. For the next 15 to 20 minutes we'd be viewing the horizon for seagulls and jumping sardines. Then came the task of setting up the lines, weights and reels, and it was essential that this was done properly – if you lost a fish, it was viewed as a catastrophe.

We would proceed at about 8 to 11 knots, going round in large circles, and, sure enough, Claudio would reel in an enormous tuna. The girls on the boat would be impressed and then shriek in disgust as he gutted the fish there and then (tuna is a warm-blooded fish and needs to be bled as soon as you catch it). Claudio would swear he was one of the finest fishermen in Greece, but since he was Neapolitan and not Greek, he felt it only right that he should give two-thirds of his catch to the local fishermen on the pier or the captain of a passing boat.

One thing's for sure, in order to off-load the quantities of tuna that Claudio insisted on catching, we had regular tuna dinners, with Dave drafting in the diners, so that no fish went to waste. Here is my favorite of many tuna recipes I had to discover.

Firstly make the dry marinade by mixing all the ingredients together on a baking sheet. Place it to one side.

Cut the tuna fillet in half lengthwise and then cut each length in half lengthwise again, so you have 4 long strips of meat. Cut each strip across into 6 cubes per strip.

Now cut the lemons in half lengthwise and then cut 6 wedges out of each lemon. Toss in a bowl with a teaspoon of olive oil and a pinch of salt. Turn on your broiler if your barbecue isn't fired up yet. Sit the lemon wedges on a sheet of aluminum foil and broil on a moderate heat for at least 5 minutes on each side, until charred and softened. Remove from broiler and allow to cool.

Push cubes of tuna on the rosemary stalks or skewers, followed by wedges of cooked lemon – you should get 4 cubes of tuna and 3 wedges of lemon per skewer. The remaining broiled lemons will be used to dress the pepper salad. Roll each skewer through the dry marinade, put them on a plate and they are ready to be barbecued. I suggest you prepare this dish a little earlier and put in the refridgerator for an hour or two.

Make the salad: add half the extra-virgin olive oil to a large bowl and throw the bell peppers in whole. Mix them vigorously and add a pinch of salt. Place the peppers on the hot barbecue, preferably when you first light it as the barbecue will be flaring and this is an opportune time to char vegetables. Turn them over and cook on all sides until blackened and slightly softened – the skins will look very wrinkled and black. Put the cooked peppers back into the oiled bowl and cover tightly with plastic wrap. This will create a steamy environment and the skins of the peppers will then come away more easily. Allow the peppers to sit for at least 20–30 minutes, then remove the plastic wrap and peel away the skins. Gently tear the peppers into pieces, discarding the seeds. Place the peeled peppers on a large plate. Strip the oregano from the stalks and chop the leaves finely. Add this to the peppers with the capers, chopped anchovy, and the remaining oil. Mix well.

Once the barbecue is settled, broil the tuna for about 3–4 minutes on all 4 sides and place the skewers over the pepper salad. Cut the tomatoes in quarters and squeeze the juice of the tomatoes over the tuna. Now squeeze over the juice of the spare lemon wedges, season with salt and pepper and tuck in.

1 whole tuna fillet, about 1½ pounds

3 lemons

1 tablespoon olive oil

salt and pepper

6 long firm rosemary stalks (or 6 kebab skewers)

for the dry marinade

1 teaspoon crushed or ground fennel seeds

½ teaspoon ground cumin

1 teaspoon dried oregano

1 teaspoon ground coriander seeds

1 teaspoon celery salt

for the red pepper salad

about 8 tablespoons extra-virgin olive oil (Cretan is wonderful)

8 red bell peppers

5 good sprigs of oregano

1 tablespoon drained capers (preferably the tiny ones)

2 anchovy fillets, chopped

2 beef tomatoes

Makes 6 skewers

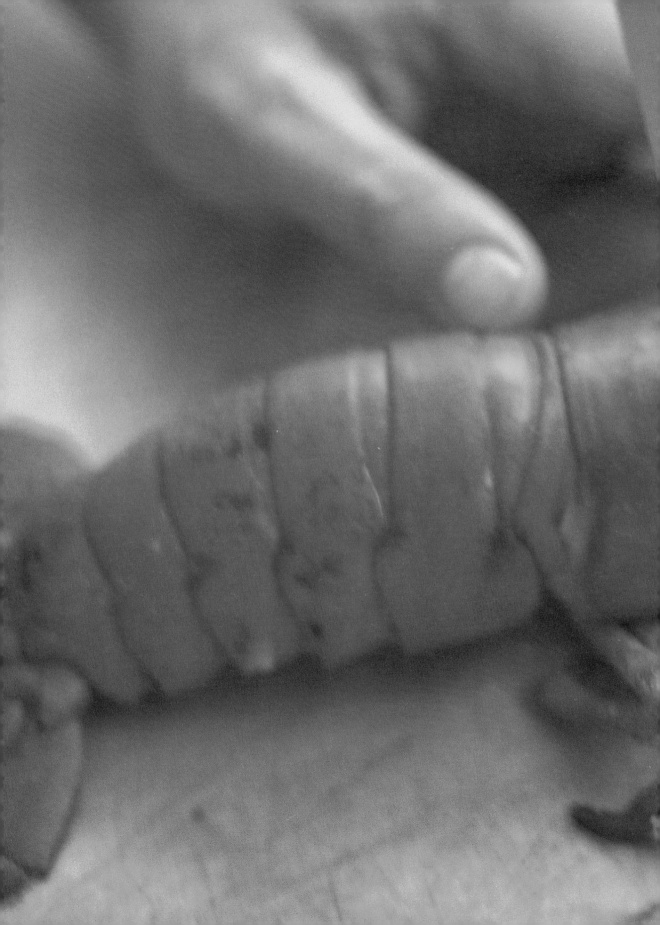

grilled lobster
with beurre maître d'

Generally you find a 1 pound lobster is a decent offering for one person. Personally I prefer buying the larger 2 pound lobsters and serving half per person, as the larger lobsters tend to be more succulent and juicy for barbecuing. Although we are going to broil the lobster, it is best to pre-boil the live lobsters. Always try to buy lobsters live, as anything else may have been previously frozen. If live ones are unavailable, use cooked lobsters and pick up the recipe later on.

Mix the butter, parsley, garlic, paprika, lemon juice, and mustard in a bowl and place to one side.

Cook the lobsters as above. When they are cool enough to handle, wet a dish towel, wring it out and place it flat on a surface next to the sink. Now place your chopping board on top. Remove the claws from the lobster. Holding the lobster firmly and using a sharp chopping knife, cut through the center of the head, pushing through the lobster lengthwise, chopping it in half through the body. Now turn the lobster round and cut lengthwise again through the tail (see pages 108–9).

At the restaurant, we crack the claws by smashing the back of a knife against the top edge of the claws, but I don't recommend you try this at home. A safer way of cracking claws (and I strongly recommend this method) is to use either nut crackers or a pair of pliers, cracking roughly around the claws, cutting away the lower part of the claws and cutting these into halves.

Cracking the lobster shell allows the heat in during broiling. Scoop the meat out from the head of the lobster into a bowl and gently heat one cube of butter from the mixture in a skillet over a low heat. Add the lobster head meat and cook for 3 minutes. Add the brandy and allow to simmer until it has all evaporated. Pour the contents of the pan into a blender, add a good pinch of salt and a good twist of pepper and blend for 20–30 seconds. Now add the parsley, garlic and butter mixture and blend together for an additional 30 seconds. Scrape the contents of the processor out with a spatula out into a bowl, ensuring they are well blended.

Using the back of a spoon, smear the flavored butter all over the flesh, tail, arms, and claws of the lobster. Broil on the barbecue, cooking the claws on all sides and the tails shell side down for about 10 minutes. Serve with baked potatoes and coleslaw, and a pint of chilled beer. Heaven...or as near as I'll get.

To kill a lobster as humanely as possible: two-thirds fill with water the largest saucepan you have that has a lid, add a teaspoon of salt, replace the lid and bring to a vigorous boil. Remove the lid, drop the lobster in and replace the lid straight away, this will ensure the lobster will be killed immediately on contact with the water. Cook the lobster for 4 minutes only, remove and allow to cool. Do not run the lobster under cold water as you will wash away the flavor. Repeat this process individually for each lobster, as trying to cram the lobsters in all at once will lower the water temperature too much, so preventing the lobsters swift dispatch and making the meat tough and leathery.

Putting a damp dish towel under your chopping board like this ensures that your chopping board will not slide about while you are manhandling the lobster.

4 ounces (1 stick) unsalted butter, cut into small cubes

a small bunch of flat-leaf parsley, finely chopped

1 garlic clove, finely chopped

½ teaspoon paprika

juice of ½ lemon

½ teaspoon English mustard

2 large lobsters, see above

1 tablespoon brandy

salt and pepper

baked potatoes and coleslaw, to serve

scallops
with orange rind, thyme, & grilled leeks

For this dish, it is best to buy live fresh scallops in the shell, then take them home to shell and clean. If scallops are not available in the shell, buy fresh cleaned scallops from the fish merchant and ask for the rounded part of the shell, because it is in these that you are going to cook the scallops. This is a lovely simple dish with ancient affiliations. You are using the shell as your skillet and cooking on an open fire.

First prepare the leeks: bring a large saucepan of salted water to a boil. While it is heating, cut off the upper green parts of the leeks and discard or keep for soups and broths. Cut the remaining parts of the leek in half lengthwise and then cut these halves again in half lengthwise, so you have 4 strips per leek. Wash the strips thoroughly and then boil them for 3 minutes. Drain them well and dry the pieces between clean dish towels or paper towels. Place in a bowl and toss with the olive oil.

Broil the leeks on the preheated hot barbecue for about 3 minutes, turn and cook the other sides for the same time. Remove and chop roughly, put back in a large bowl with a touch of lemon juice and a glug of olive oil, toss and put aside to serve later.

Prepare the scallops: in a large mixing bowl, mix the chopped thyme leaves with the garlic, good pinch of salt and the orange rind. Add the shelled scallops and olive oil, and mix gently with your fingers. Cut the French stick into 16 thin slices.

Place the scallop shells over the barbecue and leave for at least 2 minutes to heat up. Put 2 scallops in each shell and leave to cook for 5–7 minutes, until nut-brown, spooning any remaining orange rind mixture over the scallops while they cook.

Once they are cooked, carefully remove from the shells and put on a plate, leaving the shells on the barbecue. Place a slice of the French bread on each shell and press down gently with the back of a spoon, so that it soaks up the juices remaining in the shell. Put a teaspoon of leek over the bread, place the scallops back on top and cook for a further 2 minutes.

Remove the filled shells from the barbecue and serve on a large dish.

16 large scallops (see left)
a bunch of thyme, leaves stripped from stalks
½ garlic clove, finely chopped
finely shredded rind of 2 oranges
2 tablespoons olive oil
1 long French stick

for the leeks
salt
6 leeks
4 tablespoons olive oil
salt and pepper

spiedinos of scallops,
cod, & pancetta

This is a delicious Tuscan barbecued dish in which the juices of the pancetta are absorbed by the bread, which cooks to become crisp. Fennel sticks make wonderful fragrant skewers for this dish. The spiedinos go well with fresh beans, lentils, broiled vegetables, or a simple tomato and basil salad.

Strip the cod from the bone, so you have two fillets about 10 ounces, then cut each fillets into 6 cubes. Cut the ciabatta in half and then into large chunks (you will need 12 chunks in all).

Put the ciabatta chunks in a large mixing bowl, pour over the olive oil and stir around well. Remove each chunk of bread and wrap a strip of pancetta around it. Then taking a skewer, first spear one piece of wrapped bread (skewering the pancetta-wrapped side to ensure it doesn't fall off during cooking), then spear a scallop through the coral and then the white meat lengthwise, then skewer a chunk of cod. Repeat this until you have 6 pieces, 2 of each ingredient on each skewer.

Lightly season the spiedinos, place on the hottest part of the barbecue and broil for 10 minutes on each side. Serve on a large plate with a squeeze of lemon juice.

Turn the spiedinos over using a fish slice or metal spatula, as trying to do this by hand or with tongs will probably rip the meat.

Throwing some fennel stems on the coals as you are cooking helps to flavor the skewers even more and makes a wonderful aroma. If you can't get fennel sticks, try lemon grass stalks, which are now sold by many good supermarkets. They will give an exotic lemony hint to the seafood.

2 pounds cod tail

1 ciabatta loaf (if you want to make it yourself, see page 224)

4 tablespoons extra-virgin olive oil

12 slices of pancetta or smoked bacon

6 stout fennel sticks or long long skewers (about 10 inches long)

12 shelled scallops, preferably with their corals

salt and pepper

juice of 1–2 lemon(s), to serve

Makes 6 skewers

salad tropicale

You can also add salad leaves to this recipe or noodles or veg shavings to beef up the dish.

Remove the stalks from the cilantro, discard any woody sections and chop the stalks finely for the dressing.

Make the dressing: in a bowl, mix all the ingredients with the finely chopped cilantro stalks. Chill in the refridgerator while you prepare the salad.

To make the salad: first peel the mango and cut it into slices around the central stone. Cut the papaya into quarters, scoop out the seeds, then cut the papaya away from the skin, as you would a melon. Add the pieces of fruit to a bowl. Cut the palm hearts into bite-sized pieces and add them to the fruit. Add the small shrimp to the bowl, then stir in the cilantro leaves and scallion. Pour over the dressing and toss the salad.

Pour into a serving dish, scatter the large shrimp over the top and garnish with lime halves.

a small bunch of cilantro

1 mango

1 papaya

14 ounce can of palm hearts, drained

7 ounces small peeled shrimp, plus 12 large peeled shrimp, to garnish

a small bunch of scallions, thinly sliced

lime halves, to garnish

for the dressing

finely shredded rind and juice of 1 lime

1 tablespoon soy sauce

½ fresh red chile, seeded and finely chopped

1 garlic clove, finely chopped

1 teaspoon freshly shredded ginger

3 tablespoons vegetable oil

pulp from 1 passion fruit

½ teaspoon sugar

fresh cod
with chorizo sausage

In its native country, the Spanish chorizo sausage is often served with cod. Being a very flaky fish, cod is extremely difficult to broil as a fillet and is best bought as a whole fish and cut into steaks or, as in this recipe, wrapped in aluminum foil and cooked on the barbecue.

Tear off 8 sheets of aluminum foil, each about A4 size. Fold each piece of aluminum foil in half, brush the top with olive oil and then season with salt and pepper. Drizzle a teaspoon of sherry on each and place a couple of slices of chorizo sausage on top of that, followed by a fillet of fish. Fold in the edges around the fish to create a cup or boat shape around the cod. Now add another couple of slices of chorizo on top of each piece of fish, a drizzle of olive oil, salt and pepper, and one sliced cherry tomato on each. Place the cod boats around the edge of the preheated hot barbecue and cook for 20–30 minutes, until the flesh flakes readily. When the fish is cooked, slide the fillets off the foil with all the juices and other ingredients. This dish is great served with Barbecued Cabbage and potato salad.

8 tablespoons olive oil

salt and pepper

8 teaspoons Amontillado or any dry sherry

8 ounces chorizo sausage, thinly sliced

8 cod fillet steaks, each about 6 ounces

8 cherry tomatoes

Barbecued Cabbage (see page 121 and potato salad, to serve

Serves 8

grilled swordfish

Soak the cous cous in boiling water according to the instructions on packet and place in a bowl to one side.

Make the marinade/dressing: finely chop the marjoram or oregano and grind together with the salt. Add the chopped red chile and grind this in as well. Put the ground mixture into a bowl, add the finely chopped tomatoes and stir the mixture well with a spoon. Now add the vinegar and olive oil, stir all the ingredients together and place to one side.

Using a sharp knife, cut the fish with into slices about 2 inches wide. Put these in a large dish and spoon over one-third of the marinade/dressing. Turn to coat well. Allow the fish to sit in this mixture for a couple of minutes.

Meanwhile, finish preparing the cous cous. Finely chop the cucumber and very finely chop the red onion. Add these to the warm cous cous, pour in the remaining marinade/dressing and stir through thoroughly.

Remove the swordfish from the dish and broil on the preheated hot barbecue for 1 minute on each side. Serve the swordfish on top of the cous cous with a good squeeze of lemon juice.

1½ pound fillet of swordfish

juice of 1–2 lemons, to serve

for the marinade/ dressing

bunch of fresh marjoram or oregano

½ teaspoon Maldon salt or a good pinch of fine salt

1 red chile, seeded and finely chopped

2 tomatoes, finely chopped

2 teaspoons white wine vinegar

5 tablespoons extra-virgin olive oil

for the cous cous

9 ounces easy-to-make cous cous

½ cucumber

½ red onion

Serves 6

chicken spago

This dish comes originally from the celebrated Spago restaurant in Sunset Boulevard, Los Angeles, and is one of the most wonderful ways of cooking with chicken.

First make the stuffing: bring a small saucepan of water to a boil. Smash the garlic bulb into individual cloves and boil them, with the skin on, for 15 minutes. Drain through a strainer and allow to cool. Peel the husks from the garlic and mash the cloves in a mixing bowl. Add the parsley, followed by the olive oil, lemon juice, salt and pepper, and mix well.

Lay the chicken portions on a chopping board, skin side down. Stuff the garlic and parsley between the meat and the skin of the breast and leg of each piece of chicken. Place on a baking sheet and put in the refridgerator until you are ready to cook.

To cook the chicken, place on the preheated hot barbecue and cook for 7–10 minutes on each side. Alternatively use a griddle pan or ordinary broiler preheated to moderate-to-high for the same amount of time.

Serve with a wedge of lemon, green beans, and boiled potatoes.

2 corn-fed chickens, each about 2 pounds, with the backbone removed, but the leg and breast held together, to give 4 half portions (if possible, get this done for you by the butcher)
1 lemon, cut into wedges, to serve

for the stuffing
1 large head of garlic
2 bunches of flat-leaf parsley, finely chopped
2 tablespoons olive oil
juice of 1 lemon
salt and pepper

Caribbean Connoisseur, Florida (www.caribcob.com) sells jerk seasoning and other Caribbean products online.

jerk chicken

It's probably easier to get jerk seasoning ready-mixed as it is now available from better supermarkets and good food shops. You will need about 6 tablespoons.

Mix the jerk seasoning ingredients together in a saucepan, add 4 tablespoons of the corn oil and heat gently until the seasonings are well mixed and aromatic. Pull from the heat and allow to cool.

Take the chicken and make 4 slits along each leg and 4 deep slits along each breast. Rub two-thirds of the seasoning all over the chicken and place on the preheated hot barbecue.

Put the remaining jerk seasoning in a small saucepan, pour over the remaining corn oil and mix well. Occasionally brush the cooking chicken with the oil and jerk mixture. Ensure the chicken is well cooked, and once you think it is done (which should take least 30 minutes), slow-cook it around the edge of the barbecue for a further 20 minutes, which will make it sweeter, stickier and the meat will fall from the bone. The total cooking time should be about 50 minutes in all. Don't cook the chicken while the barbecue is flaring, but wait until the coals have bedded in a bit and are glowing hot, as this ensures that the chicken cooks through to the bone.

Jerk chicken is best served with barbecued corn on the cob, plantain (see below) and coleslaw.

4 legs and 4 breasts of chicken on the bone

4 fluid ounces (½ cup) corn oil

for the jerk seasoning

1 teaspoon dried or chopped fresh thyme

2 teaspoons celery salt

1 teaspoon garlic salt

1 teaspoon cayenne pepper

1 teaspoon ground coriander seeds

1 teaspoon ground turmeric

2 teaspoons ground allspice

1 teaspoon onion powder

1 teaspoon lemon pepper

2 teaspoons ground black pepper

bunch of chives, finely chopped

finely shredded rind of 1 lemon

barbecued plantains

2–3 plantains
2 pinches of dried chiles
2 pinches of granulated sugar
2 tablespoons vegetable oil
juice of 1 lime

Steam the plantains in their skins for 20 minutes. Pat dry, peel, and cut in half lengthwise. Mix together the chiles, sugar, and a little oil. Brush this over the plantains, then broil on the preheated hot barbecue for 5–7 minutes on each side with a squeeze of lime juice.

barbecued cabbage

Cook the cabbage whole in a large saucepan of boiling salted water for 10 minutes, remove from the boiling water and leave to drain stalk-side up.

In a bowl, mix the bacon with the sugar, a good pinch each of salt and pepper, and the olive oil. Cut the cabbage into 4 and toss the pieces in the oil and bacon mixture. Then wrap them in pieces of aluminum foil, ensuring each wrap has bacon in it.

Place around the edges of the coals and ashes of the preheated hot barbecue and cook for 1 hour.

1 large cabbage
salt and pepper
4 slices of bacon, finely chopped
a good pinch of granulated sugar
a good glug of olive oil

beef carpaccio

Although beef carpaccio is often considered hard to prepare at home, this way – using plastic wrap and a rolling pin – it isn't. You need about 3 ounce beef fillet, about ½ inch thick, per person. It is probably best to buy one large piece and slice it.

Take 2 large pieces of plastic wrap about 12 inches square and lay them out flat. Drizzle a small amount of olive oil and a twist each of salt and pepper over one piece. Place the beef medallion in the center of the oiled plastic wrap and cover with the other piece. Using a rolling pin, gently pound the meat until it is softened and then roll the beef as thinly as possible, every now and again pulling the plastic wrap flat between rolling.

Once you have the beef as thin as you can get it, pull off the top layer of plastic wrap and put a plate top-side down on the beef, turn the plate over with the beef and plastic wrap, then remove the plastic wrap. Drizzle a little more olive oil over the beef and repeat the process as many times as necessary.

To serve, add anything from arugula and Parmesan with a little balsamic vinegar to mixed fried mushrooms with lemon and black pepper, Oriental Teriyaki Dressing (page 45) with shiitake mushrooms, or a spoonful of broiled vegetables.

Being traditionally an American dish, barbecued ribs go well with coleslaw, jacket potatoes, and onion rings.

dorchester spare ribs

Although you can buy ribs raw and pre-marinated, making your own marinade will definitely help you stand out in the barbecue stakes.

Well ahead, make the marinade by mixing all the ingredients together thoroughly in a large mixing bowl. Add the ribs to the marinade, mix well and allow to marinate for at least an hour, but preferably overnight.

Broil the ribs slowly around the edges of the hot barbecue for 15–20 minutes on each side, until a deep reddish brown. Slow cooking will mean that the meat falls from the bone easily when you bite into it.

16 pork spare ribs

for the marinade

4 fluid ounces (½ cup) tomato ketchup

4 fluid ounces (½ cup) HP Sauce

juice of 1 lime

dash of Tabasco sauce

5 tablespoons cola

good dash of Worcestershire sauce

shake of celery salt

1 garlic clove, finely chopped

small bunch of cilantro, chopped

2 tablespoons olive oil

good twist of pepper

slow-roasted marinated loin of pork

This is a version of a traditional Tuscan dish, where a shoulder of pork is roasted slowly in milk with lemon juice and fresh herbs.

The day before, cut the pork loin in half lengthwise and then in half again the same way to give you 4 strips. Place to one side.

Make the marinade: add the olive oil to a large saucepan, together with the whole cracked cloves of garlic, all the herbs (left whole), the mustard, and the ground fennel seeds. Heat gently, add the wine and bring to a boil. Reduce by half and pull from the heat. Add the lemon rind and juice and place the pork in the pan. Pour over all the milk, cover and allow to marinate in the refridgerator overnight.

Next day, remove the pork from the marinade and place on a dish. Place the marinade mixture in a saucepan over a very low heat and let it simmer gently for 40–50 minutes.

To cook the pork: cook for 15 minutes on each side over a preheated medium-hot barbecue, occasionally drizzling a small quantity (a teaspoonful) of the reduced marinade over the pork (a pastry brush is the best tool to use for this).

To serve, slice the pork roughly and drizzle over the reduced marinade. This goes really well with wet or broiled polenta (see page 131) and a fresh salad.

3 pound loin of pork (skin off)

for the marinade

1 tablespoon olive oil

2 garlic cloves, cracked but left whole

a sprig of rosemary

a sprig of thyme

a sprig of sage

1 bay leaf

1 tablespoon grainy or Dijon mustard

½ teaspoon ground fennel seeds

½ glass of white wine

finely shredded rind and juice of 2 lemons

1 pint (2½ cups) full-fat milk

Serves 8

Make sure you have a sharp knife for the preparation here, although it is more confidence that is required than butchery skills, and it is, in fact, very easy to prepare.

marinated lamb steaks

This recipe cooks superbly whether on a barbecue, griddled or broiled, and once cooked the lamb can be sliced thinly and tossed into a salad, or eaten as an alternative to beef steak. Traditionally, with a French cut, the lamb would be sliced across the bone and broiled. For this recipe, though, I find that it is easier to buy a leg of lamb off the bone.

First prepare the marinade: strip the rosemary leaves from the stems and chop them as finely as you can, almost to dust. Add these to a large mixing bowl together with the garlic, balsamic vinegar, lemon juice, dried chiles, sugar, cayenne or black pepper, salt, and olive oil. Mix all the ingredients together and place the marinade to one side.

Put the lamb leg on a chopping board and remove any string or netting holding it together. Cut it halfway through on the narrower side in order to open the joint up. Then, using the knife in a sweeping motion, cut through the fatty divides of the three sections of meat. Slice lengthwise into 6 pieces and trim each piece to remove any sinew and loose fat. Put each piece of lamb flat on the board, place the knife on the side of each steak, halfway down, and slice about two-thirds of the way through, then open up the steak and, using the knife, score gently into the meat until it lies flat. This is called 'butterflying'. Once butterflied, score the meat lightly to help absorb it the marinade.

Now place all the steaks into the marinade and mix well. Preferably leave to marinate overnight in the refridgerator, or at the very least for an hour. As it marinates, the meat will lighten slightly in color and become far more tender. The sugar and balsamic vinegar will caramelize around the lamb while cooking.

Cook the steaks on a preheated hot barbecue for about 5 minutes on either side and serve. Lamb steaks go wonderfully well with a tomato and mozzarella salad or with cous cous and Tzatsiki (page 44) with a lemon on the side.

1 whole leg of lamb, off the bone

lemon halves, to serve

for the marinade

4 long sprigs of rosemary

1 garlic clove, finely chopped

1 teaspoon balsamic vinegar

juice of ½ lemon

pinch of dried chiles

pinch of granulated sugar

pinch of cayenne pepper (if you have it – if not, a pinch of black pepper)

pinch of salt

3 tablespoons olive oil

Serves 4–6

vegetables & accompaniments

Side dishes to accompany barbecues need to be simple

and fuss-free, yet strong in flavor to match the robust

main dishes. It's very nice if they, too, can be cooked

on the barbie, like the polenta dishes that follow later

in this section, but it's probably easier if they're sitting

already prepared, happily chilling in

the refridgerator.

broiled potato salad

This dish helped launch my media career. I had been asked to cook a barbecue supper at a party for the chairman of a television station. Unfortunately, some of the produce I'd ordered wasn't delivered. After a quick whip round, all I seemed to have was an excess of potatoes. So I sliced them and cooked them on the barbecue, then dressed them. The chairman and his guests loved them and a couple of weeks later I had a call from his television company asking me to do a pilot.

First put a large saucepan of salted water on to boil for the potatoes and make the dressing by mixing all the ingredients in a large bowl and seasoning to taste.

Peel the potatoes and slice them into ¾ inch discs. Blanch these in the boiling water for 3 minutes. Drain and pat dry between dish towels. Place the slices in a large bowl or dish, drizzle over the olive oil and mix well to ensure all the slices are covered in olive oil.

Place the potato slices on the preheated hot barbecue and cook for 3–4 minutes on each side, until crispy.

Remove the potato slices from the barbecue, place in a serving dish and pour the dressing over them.

Make sure your potatoes are well dried after blanching – this stops them sticking to the barbecue once they are basted in olive oil.

When making potato salad, dress the cooked potatoes while they are still warm as they will then absorb much more of the dressing's flavors as they cool.

6 large potatoes
4 tablespoons olive oil

for the dressing

1 red chile, seeded and finely chopped

1 garlic clove, finely chopped

a bunch of flat-leaf parsley, finely chopped

2 tablespoons white wine vinegar

6 tablespoons olive oil

salt and pepper

Serves 6

panzanella

This is an Italian country salad and, as in a lot of traditional Italian dishes, it is based on the principle that nothing gets thrown away, its main ingredient being stale (not mouldy!) bread, combined with the juice of overripe tomatoes, broiled red bell peppers and some very strong flavorings like anchovies and capers. It makes a great accompaniment to broiled food, or is delicious by itself.

Preheat the oven to full whack, lightly toss the whole red bell peppers in a thin layer of olive oil and roast for about 20 minutes, turning them every 5 minutes so they are blackened on all sides. Once cooked, place in a bowl, cover with plastic wrap and leave to cool (this steams the peppers, making the skins easy to peel).

While they steam, break the bread into small chunks and add to a bowl, together with the canned tomatoes and their liquid, the fresh tomatoes, anchovy fillets, capers, garlic, vinegar, basil, remaining olive oil, salt and pepper. Mix well and chill in the refridgerator.

Now peel the skins from the red peppers and tear the flesh gently or slice into long thin strips, removing the seeds.

Transfer the bread salad to a large dish and garnish with the strips of red peppers and, if you like, thinly sliced red onion. Chill for about 1 hour, then serve.

4 red bell peppers

6 tablespoons extra-virgin olive oil

1 large stale loaf of bread, preferably Pugliese but if not a large bloomer

1 14 ounce can of chopped plum tomatoes

4 tomatoes, roughly chopped

12 anchovy fillets, chopped

2 teaspoons capers

1 garlic clove, finely mashed

2 tablespoons red wine vinegar

a bunch of basil, shredded

salt and pepper

rice & peas

The first time I made this traditional Caribbean dish I got it disastrously wrong by assuming that peas meant green peas. This is not the case and, in fact, the 'peas' they use are black-eyed or red kidney beans. It makes a delicious accompaniment for barbecued food. The rice should be slightly pink and, traditionally, you should use broth instead of water.

Heat the corn oil gently in a large saucepan, add the chopped onion and garlic, and cook until softened and translucent. Stir in the chili powder or dried chiles, allspice, and turmeric. Pour in the rice and mix together well, then add the drained beans and mix well again. Add twice as much water to the pan as there is rice, etc., together with a pinch of vegetable broth powder if you wish. Bring to a boil and cook over a moderate heat until all the water has been absorbed, about 20 minutes.

Once cooked, stir in the creamed coconut, season with salt and pepper, and mix well. Pull to one side, cover and allow to sit for at least 30 minutes before serving so that the flavors have time to infuse.

4 tablespoons corn oil

1 white onion, chopped

2 garlic cloves, chopped

a pinch of chili powder or ground dried red chiles

½ teaspoon ground allspice

1 teaspoon ground turmeric

1 pound 2 ounces American long-grain rice

2 x 14 ounce cans of red kidney beans or black-eyed peas, drained

a pinch of vegetable broth powder (optional)

7 ounces creamed coconut, shredded

salt and pepper

bruschetta

The best bread to use for this is Pugliese, as its dough contains olive oil; if not, any firm loaf will do. The basis of bruschetta is broiling the bread over the barbecue then, once crispy, rubbing with a clove of garlic, drizzling it with olive oil, and piling things up on top, whether chopped tomatoes with salt, olive oil, and basil or chopped olive tapenade, thin slices of mozzarella with red peppers, and oregano, or goat cheese and artichoke with chopped thyme. They make lovely things to eat while waiting for the fish or meat to be done, and you can cook them over hot coals while waiting for your barbecue to settle down.

polenta

The bright yellow of polenta (cornmeal) always creates spectator interest on the barbie. In southern Italy, it is a delicious source of carbohydrate, much as the potato is in the more northern territories. It is also a staple ingredient in many African diets, where it is known as ground maize.

There are two common ways of preparing polenta. One is what I call 'wet' polenta, where, once the polenta is cooked, you fold in olive oil and grated Parmesan. This is then normally served on the side as an accompaniment to meat, such as osso buco. The second way, 'dry' polenta, involves broiling the cooked polenta. Since this chapter is all about barbecuing, the broiling method is the basis of the next few recipes.

The easiest way to prepare the polenta is to follow the instructions on the packet, although I do like to add a tablespoon of olive oil once the polenta is prepared. I find that this ensures that the polenta cooks all the way through when you broil it. Once your polenta is prepared, pour it out on to a flat working surface and leave it to set for an hour, then slice it into pie-type wedges for broiling.

When the wedges are nice and firm, brush them lightly with olive oil and then cook on the preheated hot barbecue for at least 10 minutes on each side to get them nicely crisp. Be sure to try to turn or lift them from the broiler, using a spatula, only when they are well crisped, or they will break up.

Nowadays, packets of mixed 'wild' mushrooms are sold by most supermarket chains and are relatively well-priced.

polenta
with mushrooms & gorgonzola

4 tablespoons olive oil

6 shallots, finely chopped

2 garlic cloves, finely chopped

12 flat-cap mushrooms, sliced

8 ounces mixed wild mushrooms

2 sprigs of thyme, finely chopped

1 glass of white wine

12 fluid ounces (1½ cups) heavy cream

6 ounces Gorgonzola, roughly cubed

4 ounces (1½ cups) Parmesan cheese, shredded

a handful of flat-leaf parsley, finely chopped

juice of ½ lemon

1 pound 2 ounces (2⅔ cups) of polenta, prepared and broiled as described on page 131

Put the olive oil in a large wide-bottomed saucepan set over a low heat, add the shallots and garlic, and cook gently until the shallots are softened. Turn the heat up to high and add all the mushrooms, both sliced and whole wild. Cook for 4–5 minutes, stirring occasionally. Add the thyme and cook for a further minute. Reduce the heat to moderate and cook for a further 5 minutes.

Add the wine and reduce by two-thirds. Add the cream and allow to boil, stirring constantly, until the sauce is reduced by one-third, then turn the heat down to low.

Add the Gorgonzola, Parmesan, parsley and lemon juice, stirring constantly until the cheeses have melted. Serve poured over broiled polenta.

polenta
with asparagus

Melt the butter gently in a saucepan, add the shallots and garlic, and cook until the shallots are softened. Add the chopped asparagus, but not the tips, and cook for 4–5 minutes over a gentle heat. Add the wine, increase the heat to moderate and reduce the liquid by half.

Remove from the heat and mash the asparagus and shallots thoroughly with the back of a fork until smooth; alternatively, blitz in a blender until smooth.

Put the purée back over a moderate heat, and add the heavy cream together with the asparagus tips. Bring to a boil, then turn the heat down and allow to reduce by one-third.

Add the Parmesan, oregano, and salt and pepper to taste. Serve poured over the broiled polenta. Yum yum, pig's bum.

2 ounces (½ stick) butter

3 shallots, finely chopped

1 garlic clove, finely chopped

a bunch of asparagus, trimmed, tips removed and reserved, stalks finely chopped

½ glass of white wine

7 fluid ounces (¾ cup) heavy cream

4 ounces (1½ cups) Parmesan cheese, finely shredded

pinch of finely chopped fresh oregano

salt and pepper

18 ounces (2⅔ cups) of polenta, prepared and broiled as described on page 131

¼ pint (⅝ cup) extra-virgin olive oil

1 red chile, seeded and finely chopped

2 garlic cloves, finely chopped

6 anchovy fillets

2 tablespoons capers

1 stalk of rosemary, leaves finely chopped to a powder

2 x 14 ounce cans of plum tomatoes

7 ounces (2 cups) pitted black olives

1 pound 2 ounces (2⅔ cups) of polenta, prepared and broiled as described on page 131

freshly shredded Parmesan cheese, to serve

polenta
with sauce napoletana

Heat the olive oil in a saucepan over a moderate heat, add the chile, garlic, and anchovies, and cook for 1 minute. Add the capers and rosemary, stir and add the tomatoes with their liquid. Stir these in and turn to the lowest heat.

Allow to cook for at least 1½ hours, stirring occasionally. After an hour, gently break up the tomatoes with the back of a fork. After another 20 minutes, stir in the olives. When fully cooked, your sauce should be a deep rich red, with a wonderful sheen.

Serve poured over the polenta and sprinkled with Parmesan.

The quattro formaggio sauce is also delicious served on a fat slice of toast.

polenta
with quattro formaggio

½ glass of white wine

1 garlic clove, finely chopped

1 lb. 2 oz. mascarpone cheese

4 ounces Gorgonzola cheese, cut into cubes

4 ounces Tallegio cheese, cut into cubes

a small bunch of oregano, finely chopped

20 large spinach leaves, finely chopped

a pinch of freshly shredded nutmeg

2 tablespoons unsalted butter

7 oz. (3 cups) Parmesan cheese

finely shredded rind and juice 1 lemon

salt and pepper

1 lb. 2 oz. (2⅖ cups) polenta, prepared and broiled as described on page 131

Bring the wine and garlic to a boil in a large saucepan over a high heat, add the mascarpone and mix together until smooth. Reduce the heat to moderate, stirring continuously. Now add the Gorgonzola and Tallegio, and stir until they have melted. Add the oregano, spinach, nutmeg, and butter, and cook for 2 minutes. Turn the heat to its lowest possible setting and stir in the Parmesan, lemon juice, and lemon rind. Season to taste.

Serve poured over broiled polenta.

polenta
with herb salsa

Place the chopped herbs in a blender and blitz to a mash. Remove and place in a bowl. Now add the anchovies, capers, and garlic to the blender and blitz these to a paste. Add this to the herbs and stir together. Now add the mustard, olive oil, vinegar, and shredded zucchini to the bowl and stir well.

Serve over hot broiled polenta with some extra olive oil.

a bunch of mint, finely chopped

a bunch of flat-leaf parsley, finely chopped

a bunch of marjoram, finely chopped

1½ ounces of anchovy fillets

2 tablespoons drained capers

1 garlic clove, finely chopped

1 tablespoon Dijon mustard

8 fluid ounces (1 cup) extra-virgin olive oil, plus more to serve

2 tablespoons red wine vinegar

2 zucchini, shredded

18 ounces (2⅖ cups) of polenta, prepared and broiled as described on page 131

desserts

As with side dishes, the sweet course that follows a barbecue needs to be easy to make or something you can prepare well ahead. Usually something light, possibly involving fresh summer or tropical fruits, is the most likely candidate, although a nice tart always goes down well.

pineapple tarte tatin

This is a twist on the traditional apple tarte tatin.

First trim off the skin of the pineapple, then cut the pineapple into quarters. Halve these into eighths and then cut them into chunks, discarding any woody core. Place the chunks in a colander and leave to drain.

In a 12 inch skillet which has an ovenproof handle (i.e. not plastic), melt the butter with the sugar, a teaspoon of water, and the lime juice. Bring to a boil over a moderate heat and cook, stirring, for 5 minutes. Add the pineapple and cook, stirring from time to time, for a further 5 minutes. Remove the pan from heat and allow to cool, then chill in the refridgerator for 1 hour.

Roll out the pastry to a round with a diameter of about 14 inches. Remove the pan from the refridgerator and place the pastry over the top. Trim off the edges and push the pastry into and around the edge of the pan. Place back in the refridgerator to allow the pastry to rest.

Preheat the oven to 350°F. When it is hot, put the pan into the oven for 15–20 minutes, until the pastry is nicely browned. Remove from the oven and allow to settle for 20 minutes. Place a plate over the top and, using oven gloves, lift the pan and plate together and flip it over and out on to the plate. The tarte serves well with ice-cream or crème fraîche.

1 large pineapple
4 ounces (1 stick) butter
4 ounces (½ cup) superfin
sugar
juice of 1 lime
puff pastry
ice-cream or crème
fraîche, to serve

barbecued apples
with ice-cream

A really nice accompaniment for ice-cream is grilled apples and they're so simple to do.

Slice the apples into 1¼ inch thick discs, removing any core. Brush with olive oil and place on the barbecue. Broil on one side for 2 minutes, turn over and sprinkle with sugar, cinnamon, and lemon rind. Allow to cook for a further 2–3 minutes, then remove and serve.

4 large cooking apples

olive oil

2 tablespoons granulated sugar

½ teaspoon ground cinnamon

finely shredded rind of 2 lemons

thai fruit salad
with ice-cream

1 star fruit

1 honeydew melon

¼ watermelon

1 pineapple

4 passion fruit

juice of 3 limes

2 tablespoons superfine sugar

a good pinch ground chili

7 ounces shredded coconut

Cut the star fruit into 4, then into slices; cut the melon and watermelon into chunks, removing all the pips and peel. Peel, core, and chop the pineapple. Add all these to a bowl.

Cut the passion fruit into halves, scoop the insides into a separate bowl, add to this the lime juice, sugar, chili, and coconut, and mix well until the sugar dissolves.

Pour this over the fruit and mix well. Serve very chilled.

To judge whether or not a pineapple is ripe, tug at one of the inner leaves – it will come away easily if the pineapple is in the right condition.

hoot's pineapple bugles

The idea for this dessert came from a friend of mine who is named after a famous cowboy actor called Hoot Gibson.

4 baby pineapples
4 ounces desiccated coconut
6 ounces (¾ cup) granulated
sugar
2 vanilla pods
1 inch piece of fresh
ginger, finely chopped
1 red chile, seeded and
finely chopped
juice of 2 limes
4 tablespoons rum

Peel the skins off the pineapples, leaving the leaves at the top. Pour out the coconut on to a large plate or tray and place to one side.

In a saucepan, mix the sugar, seeds from the vanilla pods, ginger, chile and the lime juice. Bring to a boil and allow to simmer until the sugar is golden in color.

Dry the pineapples with a clean paper towel. Pour the hot sugar syrup into a tray and roll the pineapples one by one first in the sugar syrup and then in the coconut. Allow to set.

To serve, place on a plate covered with flaked ice, pour over the rum, and ignite.

Although, nowadays, Sundays are perhaps not quite what they were in the past, with it being to some degree just another working day for a lot of people, for the lucky ones it is still a time to laze around. It's also a good occasion to get friends together in a laid-back atmosphere for a bit of lunch. Obviously, being a chef, some of my most memorable Sundays have been spent cooking and eating this way.

As Sunday should be the day of rest, I have tried to keep the recipes in this chapter as straightforward and simple as possible, to make sure you're not spending too much time over a stove – although, I find cooking can be a wonderful way to relax and disappear into your own world of thoughts.

sunday food

poached eggs
with fried bread & boiled tomatoes

First, start by preheating the broiler, then bring 3 pints of water to a boil in a large saucepan. Place the tomatoes in the water and boil for 3 minutes. Remove and put on a plate, lightly season and drizzle over 1 tablespoon of olive oil. Put this plate at the bottom of your broiler to keep the tomatoes hot.

Put 3–4 tablespoons of olive oil in a large skillet and place over moderate heat for 2 minutes. Add the bread and fry for 3 minutes on each side (you may have to do this in two pans or in batches). Once you have cooked one side of the bread and you are turning it over to cook the other side, start to poach the eggs.

Crack each egg into a ramekin or small cup, add the vinegar to the pan of boiling water together with a good pinch of salt. When the water is boiling vigorously, using a whisk, start to stir the water clockwise very quickly until it is whirling round like a whirlpool. Quickly add the eggs, by placing the rim of the ramekin into the edge of the water and tipping the egg in, making sure the water is still boiling and whirling round. Once you've added all the eggs, the temperature of the water will reduce to perfect poaching temperature. As long as your pan is large enough, you can cook up to 6 eggs at a time, just make sure they are all pre-cracked and ready to tip into the water. Allow the eggs to cook for 45–60 seconds, then remove each egg with either a slotted spoon or a large kitchen spoon. Discard any loose egg white, the poached eggs should resemble fresh figs in shape. A little practice might be required.

Now arrange your poached eggs on top of your fried bread with the boiled tomatoes on the side and fried or broiled bacon and/or sausages if you like. Mmmmm. If you feel like it, garnish with some basil leaves.

The vinegar in the poaching water keeps the eggs in a tight compact shape.

Often when frying sausages, they tend to explode and split open. Unfortunately I have, in my time, also eaten sausages that were very charred on the outside and frighteningly pink on the inside. To avoid this, drop your raw sausages into boiling water, reduce the temperature to moderate and cook for 3 minutes. Drain, dry then pan-fry or broil as usual. This not only ensures that the sausages will be well cooked throughout, but will also make the sausages more juicy.

To ensure really crispy bacon, cook it on a low heat, taking your time.

4–8 medium tomatoes

salt and pepper

about 8 tablespoons olive oil

2–4 slices of good-quality home-cut bread, about 1 inch thick

4 eggs

3 tablespoons vinegar

fried or broiled bacon and/or sausages to serve (optional)

basil leaves, to garnish (optional)

Serves 2

A good mature Cheddar is your best bet for the cheese here, but any melting hard cheese will do.

baked eggs

This is a great dish to make when you've just jumped out of bed and you're really starving and in a bit of a rush. It's the simplest cooked breakfast you'll ever make.

Turn the oven on to full whack and smear butter over 2 small ovenproof dishes or ramekins – or, failing that, saucers. Cover each with a couple of slices of ham. Crack a couple of eggs over the top, followed by a handful of shredded cheese, and some salt and pepper. Cook in the oven for 10 minutes and tuck in. (Mind the hot plate!)

about 2 ounces (½ stick) butter

4 slices of ham

4 eggs

2 handfuls of shredded cheese

salt and pepper

croque-monsieur

8 tablespoons Béchamel Sauce (page 158)

1 teaspoon Dijon mustard

4 ounces Gruyère cheese (or Gouda, Emmenthal, Cheddar, etc.), shredded

2 egg yolks

8 slices of white bread

8 large slices of ham or 16 small

This my version of the famous French snack.

Preheat a hot broiler. In a bowl, blend together the béchamel sauce, the mustard and cheese, then vigorously mix in the egg yolks.

Toast one side of each of the slices of bread under the broiler. Once toasted, place 1 or 2 slices of ham over the untoasted side, spoon over the cheese sauce and whack under the broiler for 4–5 minutes. Serve.

american pancakes

Crack the egg into a mixing bowl and start to beat vigorously. Sift in the flours and baking powder, continuing to mix and ensuring that there are no lumps, until you have a stiff paste. Now add the butter, 8 fluid ounces of the milk, the salt, sugar, and cinnamon, continuing to stir until you have a thick batter; if it is too thick (it should just fall easily from a spoon) add a little more milk.

Gently heat a non-stick skillet and, using a tablespoon, add a dollop of mixture to the hot pan. Cook for about 1 minute on each side, until nicely colored on both sides. Serve with eggs, bacon, sausages…or with maple syrup or butter…or you name it.

1 egg

3¾ ounces (1 cup)
all-purpose flour

3¾ ounces (1 cup)
buckwheat flour

1½ teaspoons baking
powder

2¾ ounces (6 tablespoons)
melted butter

8–9 fluid ounces (1 cup)
milk

1 teaspoon salt

3 tablespoons sugar

½ teaspoon ground
cinnamon

fried or scrambled eggs,
broiled or fried bacon
and/or sausages, maple
syrup or butter, to serve

Makes about 24

If you want a nice crunchy topping to this dish, mix some breadcrumbs and finely shredded Parmesan then scatter this over the top before it goes in the oven.

tomatoes wrapped in bacon & slow-cooked in béchamel sauce

This recipe was big in my grandparents' household, as my grandad grew his own tomatoes. It is also a great dish when the cupboards are bare or you're not feeling all that flush and you need to feed family or friends – for around $10, this dish will feed 6.

Preheat the oven to 325°F. Bring a saucepan of water to a boil and blanch the tomatoes for 1 minute. Drain, allow to cool and then peel.

While the tomatoes are cooling, gently seal both sides of the bacon in a dry non-stick skillet. Wrap each of the peeled tomatoes in a slice of bacon, securing in place with a cocktail stick.

In a bowl, mix the béchamel sauce with the cheese, nutmeg, Worcestershire sauce, and mustard. Season to taste. Spoon just enough of this cheese sauce into a large oven dish to cover the bottom, then fill the dish with all the wrapped tomatoes and pour over the remaining sauce.

Bake in the oven for 40 minutes and serve. This is a perfect Sunday evening number.

18 medium-sized tomatoes

18 slices of bacon

2 recipe quantities Béchamel Sauce (page 158)

6 ounces (2½ cups) mature Cheddar cheese, shredded

a pinch of freshly shredded nutmeg

a dash of Worcestershire sauce

1 teaspoon mustard

salt and pepper

Serves 6

ricotta & spinach crêpes
with béchamel sauce

I was recently asked to judge a celebrity cooking competition between the girls and boys of the pop group Steps. This was the recipe they made and the blokes won. Considering none of them had ever cooked pancakes in their lives, it definitely goes to show it's a winner...a simple, delicious, balanced meal all in a crêpe.

Preheat the oven to 325°F.

Make the crêpe mixture by mixing together the eggs, flour, oregano, oil and salt. Whisk well, making sure there are no lumps, then add the melted butter and slowly add the milk until you have formed a smooth pancake batter.

In as large a skillet as you have, heat a little oil for frying. Start to make large pancakes that are as thin as possible, and, as they are cooked, stack them on top of one other, until all the batter is finished. Place them to one side.

Make the filling: in a skillet, cook the garlic in half the olive oil, then add the spinach leaves and fry gently until cooked through, about 3 to 4 minutes. (You may have to do this in two batches.) Tip into a strainer and allow to cool.

Heat the remaining olive oil in the wiped-clean skillet and fry the sliced mushrooms.

Once the spinach is cool, using the back of your hand, press the spinach against the sides of the strainer to remove any excess water. Put the spinach in a bowl and, using a fork, blend in the ricotta, half of the finely shredded Parmesan, salt and pepper, and a good pinch of nutmeg. Add the cooked mushrooms and blend together thoroughly.

Taking one crêpe at a time, spoon about 2 tablespoons of filling on it, then roll it up into a tube. When all of the pancakes are filled and rolled, pour about half the béchamel sauce into a large ovenproof dish to cover the base. Season. Now lay the pancakes in the dish and pour over the remaining béchamel. Sprinkle with the rest of the Parmesan, the breadcrumbs and a twist of pepper.

Bake in the oven for 30 minutes and serve.

for the crêpes

2 eggs

8 ounces (2 cups) all-purpose flour

2 teaspoons dried oregano

4 tablespoons olive oil, plus more for frying

a pinch of salt

2 ounces (½ stick) unsalted butter, melted

1 pint (2½ cups) milk

for the filling and topping

2 garlic cloves, finely chopped

4 tablespoons olive oil

14 ounces (12 cups) spinach

5 ounces mixed wild mushrooms (if not available, field or button will do), sliced

9 ounces (1 cup) ricotta

2 ounces (¾ cup) Parmesan cheese, finely shredded

salt and pepper

a good pinch of freshly shredded nutmeg

½ pint (1¼ cups) Béchamel Sauce (page 158)

2 ounces (½ cup) breadcrumbs

Makes eight 8 inch or six 12 inch crêpes

bruschetta
with ratatouille & toasted camembert

This is a great dish if you have an hour or so to kill on a Sunday afternoon. Ratatouille is simple and it keeps in the fridge for 2–3 days, so you can tuck in at your leisure. There are many variations and ingredients you can combine in this way and there's something very cosy about sitting down on a Sunday evening with a plate of toast spread with ratatouille and watching the TV. Right now, it's grey and cold outside, and pouring with rain, so this is exactly what I want – comfort food.

First prepare the ratatouille: cut the bell peppers in half lengthwise, remove the seeds and pith, and slice the flesh into thin strips. Chop the eggplant and zucchini into rough cubes. Put all of these into a large bowl.

Add the olive oil to the largest saucepan you have and place the pan over a moderate heat. Stir in the onions and garlic, then add the bell peppers, eggplant, and zucchini. Stir well and cook for about 20 minutes, stirring occasionally.

While this is cooking, pour the canned tomatoes into a bowl with their liquid and mash gently with a fork, adding the basil. Give the cooking vegetables a good stir, and once they are all nicely browned, pour in the tomatoes with 1½ glasses of water and stir well again. Place the pan on the back of the stove over a very low heat and cook for at least 1 hour.

Once the ratatouille is cooked, place it in a large serving bowl; if you cooked it in the oven, leave it in the casserole pan. Stir in the red wine vinegar.

Make the bruschetta: preheat a hot broiler, drizzle olive oil over the slice of bread and toast on both sides (if you have a griddle pan, use this to toast the bread). Spoon and gently spread the ratatouille on the top, then lay over some thin slices of Camembert cheese. Season with salt and pepper and put under the broiler for a couple of minutes. Cut into 4 to serve.

for the ratatouille

4 red bell peppers

1 large eggplant

2 zucchini

about a wine glassful of olive oil

1 large onion, finely chopped

3 garlic cloves, finely chopped

1 14 ounce can of tomatoes

a bunch of basil, shredded

1 teaspoon red wine vinegar

for the bruschetta

2 tablespoons olive oil

1 large slice of bread, ideally Pugliese

1 small round box of Camembert cheese

salt and pepper

red endive, chorizo, and potato salad

Cook the potatoes in boiling salted water for about 10 minutes.

While these are cooking, cut the cores out of the endives, trim off all the leaves and place the leaves in a large bowl. Drizzle with the 3 tablespoons of the olive oil and toss the leaves to ensure they are covered.

Drain the potatoes and, while still hot, put them in a bowl and add the finely chopped garlic, the remaining olive oil, ½ the lemon juice, and some salt and pepper. Lightly mix and place to one side to cool.

Heat a dry skillet on full heat and lightly toast the endive leaves on both sides for a maximum of 10 seconds per side, placing them in a bowl once cooked. Pour any juices left in the pan over the radicchio and squeeze over the other half of lemon juice.

Add the slices of chorizo sausage to the pan and cook on a medium heat for about 5 minutes, stirring occasionally. Add the cooked sausage to the potatoes.

Toss the endive leaves and lay them out on a large serving dish, followed by fresh basil leaves and then spoon over the chorizo and potatoes.

20 small potatoes, peeled and quartered

2 heads of red endive

9 tablespoons olive oil

1 garlic clove, finely chopped

juice of 1 lemon

salt and pepper

2 small chorizo sausages, thinly sliced

a bunch of basil, separated into leaves

Putting the oiled baking sheet under the broiler helps stop the fish from sticking to the sheet when it's cooking.

sole fillets
with white beans, garlic bread, & parmesan crust

This dish was extremely popular at Daphne's on Sundays, and I now sometimes add it to the menu at Randall's or The Ifield, where it's just as popular. So I guess you could call it a bit of a modern classic.

2 tablespoons olive oil, plus more for drizzling

12 sole fillets

salt and pepper

about 2 tablespoons white wine

1 ounce (2½ tablespoons) fried dried breadcrumbs

2 ounces (¾ cup) freshly shredded Parmesan cheese

pinch of dried oregano

juice of 1 lemon, to serve

for the beans

1 garlic clove

1 onion

2 carrots

2 tablespoons olive oil

14 ounces presoaked cannellini beans, or two 14 ounce cans of cannellini beans (get the best quality available or, if you can find them at your local deli, get the bottled beans)

1 glass of white wine

a bunch of parsley, chopped

7 ounces (¾ cup) vegetable or fish broth

First prepare the beans: finely chop the garlic, onion, and carrots, put them in a saucepan with the olive oil and cook gently. Drain but do not rinse or wash the canned or bottled beans. When the vegetables have softened, add the beans. Once all the vegetables start to simmer, add the white wine and reduce by half. Add the chopped parsley and cook for a couple of minutes, then pour in the broth. Turn down the heat to low and cook gently for about 30 minutes.

Towards the end of this cooking time, preheat a hot broiler. Sprinkle a little olive oil over a large flat baking sheet. Place the sheet under the broiler for 3 minutes to heat the oil. Remove and place the sole fillets on it. Season with salt and pepper and drizzle over a touch of olive oil and the white wine. Place the baking sheet under the broiler and cook for about 3 minutes, then remove, but keep the broiler on.

Pour the cooked vegetables into an ovenproof dish and place the sole fillets carefully over the top. In a bowl, mix together the breadcrumbs, Parmesan, and dried oregano and sprinkle the mixture over the fish fillets and beans. Place back under the broiler and cook for a further 3–5 minutes, until the topping is light golden-brown. Remove and serve with a good drizzle of olive oil and a squeeze of lemon juice.

classic fishcakes
with watercress & parmesan salad

There's a regular fishcake following at the restaurant and here's the recipe. Although preparation takes a little bit of time (you will need a good hour and a half to make them really well), it can be well worth your while if you make a load at a time as they freeze brilliantly. You can serve the fishcakes with whatever takes your fancy, but my suggestion is a watercress salad. It's not really necessary to serve much with fishcakes – you have ample carbohydrate from the potato, protein from the fish and eggs, so a light salad is the perfect accompaniment.

First make the fishcakes: peel the potatoes, cook them in boiling salted water until quite tender, drain and leave to dry in the warm pan. Bring another large saucepan of water to a boil.

While this is heating, cut the leaves away from the cilantro and parsley, and put them to one side. Once the water is boiling, add to it the cilantro stalks, parsley stalks, a few peppercorns, a pinch of salt, and a dash of vinegar, followed by the cod and the salmon. Pull from the heat, but do not drain; allow the fish to sit in the hot liquor until cool (about 20 minutes). Once cooled they will be perfectly poached.

Add the dried potatoes to a large mixing bowl (it's very important that the potatoes are dry, dry, dry), and add to this the chopped parsley, chopped cilantro, garlic, and eggs. Using a fork, start to roughly mix together, then add the paprika with salt and pepper to taste.

Drain the fish and allow to dry. Once dry, flake the fish into the potato-and-herb mixture (do this slowly to ensure no bones go into the fishcake mix). Work the fish in with a fork.

Pull out a long sheet of plastic wrap and lightly dust it with flour. Spoon half the fishcake mixture on to the plastic wrap, gently pressing down with the back of a spoon to form a large pancake shape. Dust this with flour and cover with another sheet of plastic wrap. Using a rolling pin or your hands, gently press or roll the plastic-wrapped mixture until it's about 1¼ inches thick.

Remove the top sheet of plastic wrap and, using a 3 inch diameter round cutter, cut out the fishcakes, gently easing them off the plastic wrap and onto a lightly floured tray. Repeat this process until you have used all the mixture, stacking the fishcakes on top of one another and dividing the layers with flour-dusted plastic wrap or they will stick together.

salt, pepper, and peppercorns

6 large potatoes

a small bunch of cilantro

a small bunch of flat-leaf parsley

a dash of white wine vinegar

10 ounces skinless cod fillets, bones removed and cut into pieces

10 ounces skinless salmon fillets, bones removed and cut into pieces

1 garlic clove, finely chopped

4 hard-cooked eggs, shelled, and chopped

a good pinch of paprika

flour, for dusting

olive oil, for frying

for the coating

3 eggs

½ pint (1¼ cups) full-fat milk

10½ ounces (2 cups) breadcrumbs

Makes 12

Prepare the coatings: mix the eggs with the milk in one bowl and pour the breadcrumbs into another. Working with one fishcake at a time, first dip it into the milk-and-egg mixture, then dip it into the breadcrumbs (best to rope someone in on this to create a production line – one person eggs, the other breadcrumbs – or you will be endlessly wiping your fingers), stack them up and place in the fridge.

To cook the fishcakes: heat about ½ inch of olive oil in a large skillet and fry the fishcakes until golden brown, about 4 minutes on each side. You may have to do this in two pans or batches.

To make the watercress salad: in a large bowl, toss together the watercress, bean sprouts or shredded vegetable with the soy sauce and olive oil. Sprinkle with Parmesan shavings and served on the side with lemon or lime wedges. Serve the fishcakes with the salad.

for the watercress salad

2–3 bunches of watercress

a handful of beansprouts or finely shredded raw vegetables

1 tablespoon soy sauce

2 tablespoons olive oil

Parmesan shavings, to serve

lemon or lime wedges, to serve.

A trick when roasting chicken is to ensure any ties are removed and splay the wings out away from the bird. This allows better heat distribution.

roast chicken
with seared fennel, mustard, & basil mash

For this dish, I prefer to use corn-fed chickens for their fuller flavor; a 2¼ pound chicken serves 4 people easily.

Preheat the oven to 425°F.

Make the herb stuffing: boil the garlic cloves in a small pan of water for 2 minutes and then drain. Roughly chop the sage and the peeled, boiled garlic. Then, using a fork, mash them together with the salt, pepper, and a teaspoon of olive oil.

Place the chicken on a chopping board and run your hand gently between the skin and flesh to create a pocket, then push the herb mixture under the skin. Secure the skin back down with a cocktail stick (if you don't have one, don't worry, it just means the chicken skin will recede a bit while roasting). Now rub the skin of the bird with olive oil and, if you like, place between the meat of the leg and breast anything from slices of lemon to baby tomatoes or carrots, whatever – to adds to the flavors of the chicken juices. Lightly dust the bird with celery salt and stuff any trimmings like herb stalks, onion peel, fennel tops or onions into the central cavity of the chicken.

Place the bird in a large roasting pan and roast for 30 minutes, then reduce the oven setting to 350°F and cook for a further 50 minutes to ensure the chicken is cooked thoroughly all the way through.

While the chicken cooks, prepare the seared fennel: cut the fennel bulbs into wedges (you should get 6 wedges out of each bulb). Grind the fennel seeds into a fine powder, using either a pestle and mortar, the side of a knife, or the back of a spoon. Place a large skillet with the olive oil over a high heat and add the fennel wedges. Allow the fennel to seal in the pan, ensuring that it is catching slightly against the base of the pan before turning. Cook on all sides until darkened. Add the finely ground fennel seeds, stir well, and reduce the heat to moderate. Add the wine, stirring all the fennel juices and bits stuck to the bottom of the pan together. Now add 2 glasses of water and leave this to simmer away.

Meanwhile, make the mustard and basil mash: place the drained cooked potatoes in a saucepan, add 3 tablespoons of olive oil and about 1 level tablespoon (or a little more, depending on how strong you like it) of the mustard and start to mash. Add

1 corn-fed chicken as above

olive oil, for brushing

a handful of lemon or carrot slices or baby tomatoes (optional)

1 teaspoon celery salt

½ glass of white wine

juice of ½ a lemon, to serve

for the herb stuffing

4 garlic cloves

a bunch of fresh sage or a good pinch of dried sage

salt and pepper

1 teaspoon olive oil

for the seared fennel

3 large fennel bulbs

1 teaspoon level ground fennel seeds

1 tablespoon olive oil

a glass of white wine

a knob of butter

for the mustard & basil mash

about 5 large potatoes, boiled, drained and mashed

about 3 tablespoons of olive oil

about 1 teaspoon grainy mustard

½ bunch of basil

8 fluid ounces (1 cup) of full-fat milk

the roughly chopped basil and the milk, with some salt and pepper. Continue mashing and gently bring the saucepan to a low heat, stirring occasionally until the mash is well combined, with a light fluffy speckled appearance. The starch content of potatoes varies throughout the year, so you might need to add more milk and olive oil.

Once the chicken is cooked, remove it from the oven and let it rest for about 5 minutes in the roasting pan. Turn the oven setting down to 230°F. Gently transfer the chicken to a chopping board, retaining any excess juices in the roasting pan. Place the roasting pan on the hob, add the white wine and place to one side for a moment.

Spoon the mash into a warmed serving dish. Turn the fennel up to full heat, add a knob of butter, stir well and pour into another serving dish. Season both the mash and fennel with salt and pepper and put them in the oven to keep warm.

Now put the roasting tray on the stove set to moderate heat and cook off the wine, while stirring the juices together in the pan. Add a touch of water and continue stirring, cooking until the liquid is reduced by half. While this is reducing, cut your chicken into pieces, place on a large serving dish, squeeze over with the juice of half a lemon and pour the gravy over the top. Remove your mash and vegetables from the oven and serve.

roasted pheasant
with crispy root vegetables & leeks mornay

Perhaps not as popular as it was up until the '50s, pheasant really is a very healthy source of meat, as it has all the goodness and very little fat. If well cooked, it is quite delicious. I am not a great fan of very well-hung game, and suggest it should be hung for at most 3 days in a cool dark space.

Years ago, a friend (and, at that time, flatmate) of mine returned home after a weekend shooting with a brace of pheasant and hung them in the airing cupboard. At the time, I was certain this wasn't suitable, but said friend insisted on hanging them and cooking them for us the following weekend. Throughout the week the smell was becoming increasingly overpowering. Sure enough, on Saturday we sat down to eat what I could only describe as fizzy pheasant. After not even a mouthful, my flatmate had to agree that he might have made a bit of a mistake with the airing cupboard scenario.

Fortunately, you can buy your pheasant pre-hung. This particular dish is one my mum makes, and my 4-year-old son tucked into it extremely happily the other Sunday.

First make the béchamel sauce: stud the onion half with the cloves, put it in a saucepan with the milk and bring to a gentle simmer. In another pan, melt the butter gently, then slowly stir in the flour to form a roux. Cook for about 1 minute over moderate heat, then slowly strain in the hot milk, stirring constantly to avoid lumps. When all the milk is added, finish by adding the bay leaf and mustard. Season to taste with salt, pepper, and a pinch of nutmeg, and simmer for 20 minutes.

While the sauce simmers, prepare the leeks (be sure to keep all the veg trimmings for your game broth and retain the water for blanching all the vegetables, as this will eventually form the basis of the broth): bring a large saucepan of salted water to a boil. Trim off the heads of the leeks and cut them across into ½ inch wide rounds. Wash the chopped leeks thoroughly, then blanch in the boiling water for 4 minutes.

While the leeks are blanching, peel the onions (retaining the peel for the broth) and cut them into wedges. Remove the leeks from the water with tongs or a slotted spoon, place in a colander and set to one side. Now blanch the onions in the boiling

3 pheasants

2 ounces (½ stick) butter

7 fluid ounces (¾ cup) port

a small bunch of thyme

a good sprig of fresh rosemary

9 slices of bacon

1 tablespoon olive oil

1 teaspoon redcurrant jelly, plus more to serve

for the béchamel sauce

½ onion

3 whole cloves

1 pint (2½ cups) milk

1¾ ounces (3 tablespoons) butter

1½ ounces (3 tablespoons) flour

1 bay leaf

1 teaspoon English mustard

salt and pepper

pinch of freshly shredded nutmeg

for the leeks mornay

6 leeks

2 medium onions

3 ounces Red Leicester cheese, shredded

a dash of Worcestershire sauce

for the crispy root vegetables

Roast Root Vegetables (page 84)

1 ounce Red Leicester cheese, shredded

Serves 6

Sometimes dressed game birds come ready barded with pork back fat, in which case you don't need to cover them with bacon – although it's a lot tastier.

water for 4 minutes, again removing with tongs or a slotted spoon, and add these to the drained leeks. Leave to cool. Reserve the blanching water.

To prepare the game broth: preheat the oven to 475°F. Trim the birds of their feet and wings, and reserve. In a clean saucepan, melt the butter over a moderate heat, then add all the vegetable trimmings, with the pheasant feet, wings, and giblets, and continue cooking over a moderate heat for about 20 minutes, until browned.

Meanwhile, put the root vegetables to roast as described on page 84, but sprinkling them with the cheese before putting them on the lowest shelf of the oven.

Once the vegetable trimmings, pheasant giblets, feet and wings are nicely browned, add the port and reduce by half. Then add 2 pints (5 cups) of the reserved vegetable blanching water, bring to a boil and reduce by two-thirds.

As that reduces, put the pheasants on a large roasting pan, season with chopped thyme and rosemary, and lay 3 slices of bacon over each bird. Then drizzle with olive oil and place to one side.

Finish the leek mornay: put the drained onions and leeks in a mixing bowl with the béchamel sauce, the cheese, and Worcestershire sauce. Mix well and pour into a gratin or ovenproof dish.

Put the pheasants in the oven on the highest shelf possible and the leek mornay on the bottom shelf of the oven, so you have the pheasant, root vegetables, and leeks all cooking together. After 15 minutes, reduce the oven temperature to 350°F and cook for a further 20 minutes. Remove the pheasant from the oven, turn the oven down to 325°F and leave the leeks and root vegetables in the oven until you are ready to serve.

Gently lift the pheasants off the roasting pan, allowing any juices running off the birds to fall back into the pan. On a chopping board, cut the pheasants lengthwise into halves and place the halves on a serving dish. Place the roasting pan on the stove over a moderate heat, pour in the game broth through a strainer and add the teaspoon of redcurrant jelly. Reduce the broth by two-thirds, stirring to deglaze the pan, to make a succulent game gravy.

Pour the gravy over the pheasant. Serve with the root vegetables, leek mornay, and more redcurrant jelly. Nice one, Mum.

confit of lamb shoulder
with bean cassoulet

First put an oven shelf on the lowest rung and preheat the oven to 300°F. Slice the carrots in half lengthwise and then cut them across into slices. Rinse the bulb of garlic under running water to remove any loose papery skin. Ensure that the lamb bone is cut into two at the joint.

Place a casserole dish on the stove over a moderate heat, add the olive oil and heat gently. Place the lamb in the dish, skin-side down, and cook for 5 minutes, then gently turn it over and cook for a further 5 minutes. Lift the lamb out of the casserole and place it to one side.

Add the chopped onion and carrots, and the chile to the casserole and cook gently for 10 minutes. Then add the whole garlic bulb and the balsamic vinegar (this softens and sweetens the vegetables), followed by the red wine, rosemary, and bay leaf. Over a moderate heat, reduce the liquid by half.

Pour in the drained tomatoes, reduce the liquid again by half and add the lentils and beans. Stir and add the broth, the mustard, and the bones. Bring to a simmer.

Gently place the lamb shoulder in the casserole, together with any juices that have collected around the meat. Add the lemon juice and rind, the sugar, and a good twist of salt and pepper. Cover the casserole and put it in the oven. Now relax for a couple of hours.

After 2 hours, carefully remove the casserole from the oven, lift out the lamb shoulder and put it to one side. Remove the bones from the casserole and discard. Place the casserole over a low heat to keep it nice and warm but not boiling.

Slice the lamb into strips, putting the strips back into the casserole. Once all the lamb has been added back to the pan, stir well. Serve with a ladle and accompany by a green salad.

2 carrots

1 head of garlic

1 shoulder of lamb, weighing about 2¾ pounds off the bone (but ask your butcher to give you the bones)

6 tablespoons olive oil

1 onion, finely chopped

1 small red chile

1 tablespoon balsamic vinegar

½ bottle of red wine

4 sprigs of rosemary

1 bay leaf

2 x 14 ounce cans of tomatoes, drained

4 ounces (⅔ cup) lentils (brown or green)

1 9 ounce can of cannellini beans

1 9 ounce can of borlotti beans

2 pints (5 cups) broth, preferably lamb

1 teaspoon Dijon or English mustard

shredded rind and juice of 1 lemon

½ teaspoon sugar

salt and pepper

toad in the hole
with onion gravy

This is a great dish if you're not in the mood for cooking but could eat a horse. It doesn't take long, is incredibly economical and, if you follow this recipe, quite delicious.

Preheat the oven to 350°F. Place the sausages in a saucepan, just cover with water and bring to a simmer. Once the water is simmering, pull the saucepan from the heat and remove the sausages with tongs or a slotted spoon, reserving the water. Place the sausages to one side.

In a mixing bowl, whisk the eggs and add the flour, then continue to whisk while slowly adding the milk until you have a thick batter of pouring consistency. Season.

Add the olive oil to a medium-sized deep roasting pan and place the pan on the stove over a moderate heat until the oil is hot. Add the thyme or rosemary to the oil and then pour in half the batter mixture. Let the batter cook on the stove for about 2 minutes. Turn the heat off and add the sausages evenly throughout the dish. Pour over the remaining batter mixture and place in the oven to cook for about 30–40 minutes.

While this is cooking, make the onion gravy: sweat the onions with the olive oil in a saucepan over a moderate heat. Once the onions are lightly browned, add the sugar, cook briefly, and then pour in the wine. Reduce by half, then add the beef broth and the sausage water. Rapidly boil down by two-thirds. Remove from the heat and season.

To serve: cut the toad in the hole into large pieces and pour over the onion gravy. Serve with fresh vegetables.

12 fresh sausages, from a butcher if possible

3 eggs

6 ounces (1½ cups) all-purpose flour

¾ pint (1¾ cups) milk

salt and pepper

3 tablespoons olive oil

sprig of thyme or rosemary, destalked and finely chopped

for the onion gravy

4 onions, chopped

4 tablespoons olive oil

1 level tablespoon white sugar

1 glass of red wine

½ pint (1¼ cups) beef broth

desserts

Last courses on Sundays need to be fairly traditional comfort treats. They needn't be too elaborate, just deeply satisfying. If you don't feel in the mood to make elaborate decorations like the chocolate ganache curls, then don't bother – that's the Sunday spirit.

If you like, you can make a lemon sauce for the pie by straining 3–4 tablespoons of lemon marmalade into a small saucepan, adding an equal amount of water and heating gently, stirring, until syrupy.

lemon meringue pie

Preheat the oven to 350°F and butter a 10 inch tart pan. Roll out the pastry to fit the pan, sprinkling with the shredded rind of 1 lemon as you roll. Line the tart pan with the pastry and cover with a piece of waxed paper. Cover that with baking beans or dry rice and bake blind for 15–20 minutes until lightly colored. Remove from the oven and allow to cool, turning the oven setting down to 300°F.

While the tart shell is cooling, in a small saucepan mix the apricot jam with 1 tablespoon of water and heat gently until you have a syrup (take care not to let it burn). Remove the beans or rice and paper from the tart shell and brush the pastry with the apricot syrup. Leave this to set while you make the filling.

Mix the egg yolks and superfine sugar together in a saucepan and bring to a gentle heat, then add the cream, lemon juice, and remaining rind, together with butter, stirring continuously so the mixture does not curdle. Pour the lemon mix into the cooled tart shell and place in the oven for 10 minutes. Once the tart is cooked, remove it from the oven and allow to cool.

2 ounces (½ stick) butter, plus more for greasing

1 recipe quantity of sweet pastry (page 216)

juice of 6 lemons and finely shredded rind of 4

1 tablespoon apricot jam

9 egg yolks

6 ounces (¾ cup) superfine sugar

7 fluid ounces (¾ cup) heavy cream

10½ ounces (3 cups) confectioners' sugar

for the meringue

12 ounces (1¾ cups) superfine sugar

whites of 6 eggs

While it cools, make the meringue: using a spotlessly clean bowl and whisk, put 1 tablespoon of the sugar in the bottom of the bowl, add the egg whites and beat vigorously until they are standing in soft peaks. Slowly add the remaining sugar, beating constantly, until the egg whites are standing in firm peaks.

Dust the cooled tart with confectioners' sugar, spoon over meringue mixture and place under the broiler for about 1 or 2 minutes, until the meringue browns slightly.

chocolate, pear, & almond tart

Preheat the oven to 325°F and butter a 10 inch tart pan. Peel and core the pears if fresh, then cut them into halves lengthwise. Roll out the pastry and use to line the tart pan. Prick the base of the tart with a fork several times (this stops the pastry rising through the filling).

In a large mixing bowl, mix the almonds, flour, sugar, and cubes of softened butter with your fingertips, until you have a crumble. Now add the eggs and mix well, again using your fingertips, until you have a paste. Add the vanilla essence, orange rind and shredded chocolate, and fold this mixture together.

Place the pear halves over the base of the tart shell and pour over the mixture. Bake in the oven for about 40 minutes.

While this is cooking, put the apricot jam in a saucepan with 2 tablespoons of water and heat gently to form a light syrup.

To test if the tart is properly cooked through, push in a small knife tip and remove; if nothing is sticking to it, the tart is done. Remove from the oven and lightly brush with the apricot glaze.

This tart is best served hot, with either ice-cream or custard flavored with a dash of Amaretto.

4 ounces (1 stick) softened butter, cubed, plus more for greasing

3–4 fresh pears (or canned pear halves, drained)

1 pack or recipe quantity of sweet pastry (page 216)

2 ounces. (⅓ cup) ground almonds

2 ounces (⅓ cup) slivered almonds

3 ounces (¾ cup) all-purpose flour

4 ounces (½ cup) superfine sugar

4 large eggs (or 6 small)

1–2 drops vanilla extract

finely shredded rind of 1 orange

9 ounces dark plain chocolate, shredded

1 tablespoon apricot jam

treacle sponge

1 ounce (2 tablespoons) unsalted butter

2 tablespoons golden syrup

4 ounces (1 cup) sifted all-purpose flour

1½ teaspoons baking powder

2 large eggs

4 ounces (½ cup) brown sugar

3 ounces (6 tablespoons) margarine

1 tablespoon whisky

extra syrup, thick cream or custard, to serve

Generously grease the insides of a 1½ pint oven-proof bowl with the butter and put it in the fridge for 5 minutes to firm up the butter. Remove from the fridge and add the golden syrup to the base of the bowl.

Put all the remaining ingredients in a mixing bowl and mix thoroughly. Pour into the oven-proof bowl over the golden syrup. Cover with a doubled-over piece of buttered aluminum foil, making a few pleats in the foil before pressing down firmly around the rim of basin. Tie the aluminum foil down around the rim of the bowl with string.

Place the bowl in a steamer over a large saucepan of boiling water and steam over a moderate heat for 1½ hours, ensuring that the saucepan does not boil dry. If you need to top up, use boiling water.

Once cooked, remove the aluminum foil and turn out the pudding. It is really great served with extra syrup, thick cream or custard.

chocolate tart
with curled chocolate ganache

This rich moist chocolate tart makes a perfect accompaniment to a strong cup of coffee at the end of a meal.

Sift the flour into a mixing bowl and add the sugar, butter cubes, and cocoa. Blend together, add the eggs and fold together well. Once blended to a firm paste, allow to rest in the fridge for at least 1 hour.

Once rested, using a cheese shredder, shred the pastry into the tart shell evenly over the base. Then, using your fingers, press down all over to form the base and gently shape the pastry up around the sides of the tart shell, making sure it's evenly thick all over. Finely shred over the dark chocolate and place the tart shell back into the fridge to rest for about 20 minutes.

Meanwhile, preheat the oven to 350°F and make the filling: melt the chocolate gently in a mixing bowl set over a saucepan of gently simmering water. In a separate saucepan, bring the milk, cream, and split vanilla pod to a gentle simmer, then turn the heat to low. Crack the eggs into a large heatproof mixing bowl and whisk lightly until mixed. Pull the milk and cream from heat. Continue to whisk the eggs while you pour in the milk and cream, ensuring they don't curdle (which can sometimes happen if you over-whisk). Gently fold the melted chocolate into this mixture.

Remove the tart shell from the fridge, pour in the filling and place straight into the oven. After 5 minutes, turn the oven down to 300°F, cook for 10 minutes more, then turn the oven down to 230°F and cook for a further 20 minutes. Finally turn the oven off but leave the tart in there for about 25 minutes or so. Remove when cool.

Make the ganache: melt the chocolate in a bowl set over a saucepan of gently simmering water. Once it has melted, stir in the butter, remove from the heat and allow to cool for at least 20 minutes. Whip the cream until just peaking and then mix in the brandy. Fold the cream gently into the cooled chocolate mixture, pour the mixture into a deep-sided baking pan about 8 x 16 inches and place in the refrigerator to set for about 20 minutes. Once the ganache has set, drag a dessertspoon along the top to form curls (one for each serving) and place on top of the tart. Dust with confectioners' sugar and eat. This tart serves well with a dollop of crème fraîche or heavy cream flavored with vanilla seeds, or a scoop of ice-cream, and some strained raspberry coulis for color.

7 ounces (1¾ cups) all-purpose flour

5 ounces (¾ cup) superfine sugar

5 ounces (1¼ stick) unsalted butter, cubed and at room temperature

1½ ounces (3 tablespoons) cocoa powder

2 large eggs

¾ ounce dark plain chocolate

confectioners' sugar, for dusting

crème fraîche, heavy cream or ice cream and raspberry coulis, to serve (optional)

for the filling

14 ounces dark plain chocolate

7 fluid ounces (¾ cup) milk

12 fluid ounces (1½ cups) heavy cream

1 vanilla pod, split

3 eggs

for the ganache

9 ounces dark plain chocolate

2 ounces (½ stick) unsalted butter

9 fluid ounces (1 cup) heavy cream

1 tablespoon brandy

Makes an 18 inch tart

For obvious reasons, most of the recipes in this section are devised to feed 8 people. However, I often find that no matter how much you make for parties, there never seems to be quite enough. Fortunately, almost all of these recipes are easily scaled up. Once you have decided to throw a party, you just have to make up your mind to the fact that you are going to have to spend most of the day making your array of nibbles.

You will find that a lot of your guests will continue to eat their way through the day or evening, and become incredibly thirsty, so it's always a good idea to have some fresh juices and some iced water so that they can pace themselves. It's also nice if your guests can actually remember the beautiful feast you have prepared for them the next day.

party food

Focaccia is widely available in supermarkets and from bakeries, but if you want to make it yourself, see page 225.

butterfly focaccia
with black olive tapenade, smoked mozzarella, & cherry tomatoes

People often take for granted making up a sandwich, but we all know the difference between a truly memorable sandwich and a moody one.

First make the tapenade: chop all the dry ingredients finely, mix together in a bowl with the mustard and oil and chill in the refridgerator.

Prepare the cherry tomatoes: add the olive oil to a large skillet, preferably non-stick, and heat until the pan is smoking. Bung in the cherry tomatoes and seal. After about 30 seconds, remove from the heat and season with the sugar, salt, pepper, and the juice of ½ the lemon rind for the tapenade. This intensifies and sweetens the taste of the tomatoes and makes them more juicy.

Allow the tomatoes to cool slightly, then pour them into a strainer, allowing the juices to drain into a bowl. Now shred the smoked mozzarella into the bowl of tomato and olive oil juices. Add the shredded basil and mix well.

Preheat the broiler to full heat, cut the focaccia in half horizontally, place both halves on a baking sheet and lightly toast the insides. Spread both halves of the focaccia with tapenade and sprinkle with the shredded mozzarella mixture on both halves. Quickly flash under the broiler just to melt the mozzarella. Leave the broiler on.

Spoon the tomatoes over the center of one half of the bread, squidging with a fork and leaving about an inch clear around the edge. Sandwich the two pieces together and cut in half lengthwise, then cut these pieces evenly across into four, giving you 8 pieces in all. Just before serving, flash again under the broiler for a moment.

a container of cherry tomatoes

2 tablespoons olive oil

a pinch of sugar

salt and pepper

1 whole smoked mozzarella cheese

2–3 basil leaves, shredded

1 focaccia loaf, about 10½ ounces

for the tapenade

1 medium-sized red chile, seeded

7 ounces (2 cups) pitted black olives

finely shredded rind of 1 lemon

½ bunch of parsley

1 garlic clove

2 canned anchovy fillets

1 teaspoon drained capers

1 teaspoon Dijon mustard

2 tablespoons olive oil

Serves 8

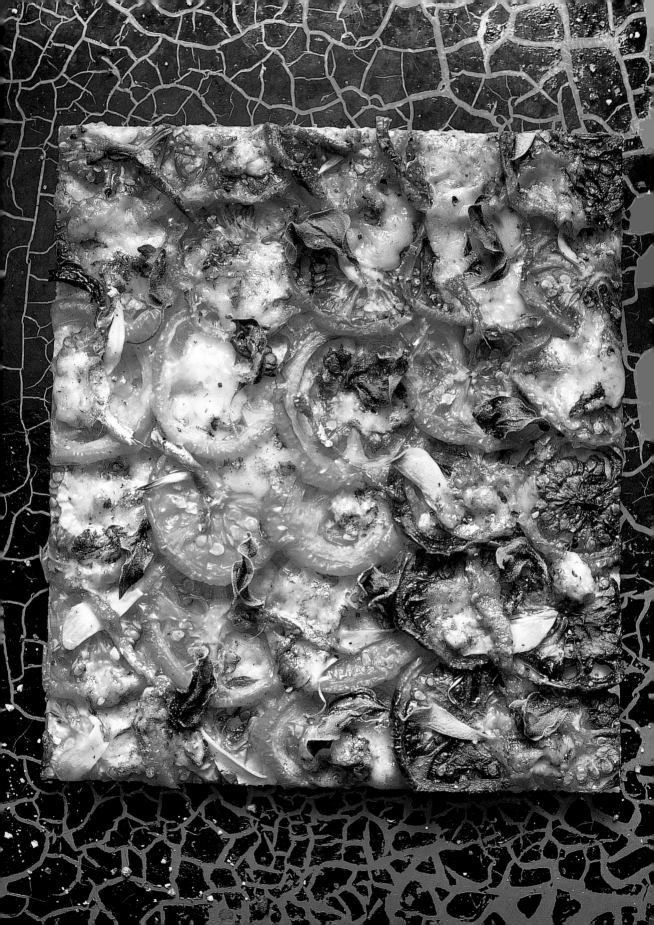

tomato & gorgonzola pissaladière

This is a really simple version of a traditional French style of pizza.

Preheat the oven to 300°F and drizzle a little olive oil over a baking sheet. Place the tomatoes slices on the oven sheet and place a slice of garlic on each slice of tomato. Season with sugar, salt, and chopped oregano. Place in the oven and cook for 30 minutes, then turn the oven setting down to 230°F and cook for a further 10 minutes. Remove from oven and place to one side.

Turn the oven setting up to 400°F and flour a work surface. Roll out the puff pastry, flouring and turning occasionally until you have a large enough square to fit your baking tray that is no less than 1¼ inches thick and about 14 inches square. Sprinkle the baking sheet with a little olive oil and a pinch of salt and place your pastry onto the tray (do this by rolling the pastry around your rolling pin and then unrolling it over your baking tray). Using a fork, spike the whole surface of the pastry. Whisk together the egg and milk, and brush the surface of the pastry with the egg wash.

Flash the pastry in the oven for 5 minutes, whip it out and then, using a spatula, lay your tomatoes out flat along the pastry in rows. Crumble a lump of Gorgonzola over each slice of tomato, and on top of this place a basil leaf. Drizzle with olive oil and sprinkle with black pepper. Put back in the oven and cook again for 10 minutes. Remove, slice into small oblongs, and serve.

olive oil, for drizzling

8–10 medium tomatoes, thinly sliced

3 garlic cloves, very thinly sliced

a pinch of sugar

salt

a bunch of fresh oregano, finely chopped

flour, for dusting

14 ounces puff pastry

1 egg

¼ pint (⅔ cup) milk

9 ounces (1¾ cups) Gorgonzola cheese

a bunch of fresh basil

black pepper

Makes 8

calamari frites
with palm heart & papaya dressing

To make this recipe you need to deep-fry – I hear alarm bells ringing, but do not worry. You'll be fine if you follow the four basic safety steps for cooking with large quantities of oil, as above:

First prepare palm heart & papaya dressing: peel the papayas, cut them in half and scoop out the seeds. Chop the papaya flesh into small cubes. Heat the olive oil in a saucepan and add the papaya. Heat through gently for 30 seconds, then remove from the heat. Slice the palm hearts as thinly as you can and mix in with the papaya. Add the garlic, chopped chile, sugar, lemon juice, and a pinch of salt. Mix together well and pour into a serving jug.

Make the batter (you need two spotlessly clean mixing bowls and a whisk): wrap a dish towel around the base of a mixing bowl with the egg yolks in it and start to beat the yolks. As you are whisking, start sifting half the flour into the yolks to form a paste. Try to get as much air into this batter mix as you can. Add the milk and the ice cubes, then continue whisking and sift in half of the remaining flour.

Using a clean whisk, whisk the egg whites until extremely fluffy (shaving foam consistency.) Pour the egg whites over the batter and very, very gently fold them in – 3–4 times, that's all!

Ensure your squid are properly cleaned and slice the tubes into rings. Lay out as many as you can on a large tray and dust with the remaining flour and season with salt. Clear both surfaces and ensure that this task has your whole concentration for the next 10 minutes, even if this means taking your phone off the hook!

1 Ensure that the extractor fan over your stove is on or open the nearest window.
2 Ensure that your cooking pan is completely dry before adding your oil.
3 Only fill your saucepan halfway.
4 Heat the oil on a moderate heat until the surface of the oil is shimmering.

Now gently immerse the calamari in the batter 5–10 at a time. Take out, drain off any excess batter and immediately drop into the hot oil, one by one, and cook for about 4–5 minutes until nicely colored. Using a fork, pick out each ring and place it on paper towel to drain. Repeat until all your calamari are cooked.

To serve, pile up your calamari and pour over your dressing, with a squeeze of lime.

1 pound squid tubes

vegetable oil, for deep-frying

deep-fried parsley sprigs, to garnish (optional)

limes, to serve

for the palm hearts & papaya dressing

3 papayas

3½ fluid ounces (⅓ cup) olive oil

1 can 12–14 ounce of palm hearts

1 garlic clove, finely chopped

1 red chile, seeded and finely chopped

1 level teaspoon sugar

juice of 1 lemon

salt

for the batter

6 eggs, separated

8 ounces (2 cups) all-purpose flour

¼ pint (⅔ cup) full-fat milk

a wine glassful of ice

Makes about 50 rings

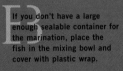

pickled salmon
with dill & mixed peppercorns on rye with mustard mayonnaise

2 pound salmon fillet, skinned and bones removed

a pinch of salt

a pinch of sugar

juice of ½ lemon, plus lemon wedges to serve

1 loaf of rye bread

for the marinade

a bunch of fresh dill

2–3 strips of lemon peel

handful of flat parsley leaves

2 onions, thinly sliced

2 carrots, thinly sliced

2 bay leaves

¾ ounce (2 tablespoons) mixed peppercorns, drained if necessary

1 teaspoon salt

black pepper

1 teaspoon sugar

2 glasses of clear malt vinegar

2 glasses of white wine

for the mustard mayonnaise

2 egg yolks

5 tablespoons vegetable oil

1 tablespoon Dijon mustard

1 teaspoon sugar

1 teaspoon white wine vinegar

Serves 8

This dish comes from Denmark, where I spent Christmas one year as a child and, although at the time I was very disappointed at not having a traditional Christmas, it developed my interest in the smörgåsbord. Mind you, when it's minus 25 and you are too young to drink schnapps, smörgåsbord was the high point of my day, and I learnt how to make every single dish. Rye bread is available from most supermarkets and bakers. It usually comes pre-sliced.

Ideally the day before, start the marinade: gently pick the dill leaves from the stalks, place the leaves to one side and finely chop the stalks. Place these in a large mixing bowl, add the parsley, lemon rind, onions, carrots, bay leaves, peppercorns, salt, a good twist of black pepper, and the sugar, and allow to stand for 10 minutes.

Using a sharp knife, slice the salmon as you would bread, into 1½ inch wide slices. Lightly dust the salmon slices with a pinch of salt and a pinch of sugar, followed by a good squeeze of lemon juice.

Now finish the marinade by adding the vinegar and the white wine. Pour half the marinade into a sealable container, add the salmon and pour the rest of the liquid over the top. Ensure that all the ingredients are beneath the liquid marinade. Seal the container and leave in the fridge for at least 12 hours.

Make the mustard mayonnaise: finely chop half the reserved dill leaves and keep the rest for garnishing. Place the egg yolks in a blender and blend for 2 minutes, then continue blending while slowly adding the oil. Once all the oil is blended in, if your mixture is too thick (you are aiming for a thickish pouring consistency), add a little warm water. Stir in the mustard, sugar, vinegar, and chopped dill leaves. Pour into a bowl, cover, and chill.

To serve: spread a slice of rye bread with a thin layer of the mayonnaise, followed by 2 slices of drained salmon. Cut the bread lengthwise into 2 fingers and repeat until you have at least 20 fingers of rye laid out on a serving plate. Now feel free to dress the salmon and rye fingers with some of the vegetables from the marinade. The easiest way to garnish is to get yourself a disposable piping bag (which you can pick up at your local supermarket), fill it with mayonnaise, snip the end of the bag with a small knife and then pipe a blob of mayonnaise on each finger. Garnish each with a reserved sprig of dill. Serve with lemon wedges.

When making the sauce, if you don't have a blender, use a sharp knife, hand whisk and bowl.

Don't leave the blini mixture to rise any longer than 2 hours, or the blinis will taste over-fermented.

homemade blinis
with salmon tartare & sauce gribiche

First make the sauce gribiche: halve the hard-cooked eggs and separate the yolks from the whites. Put the raw egg yolks in a blender with the shallot and garlic. Whiz briefly then, with the machine still running, add half the hard-cooked egg yolks and the vinegar. After these, start to add the oil in a slow steady stream. Once all the oil is added and the mixture has emulsified, add the mustard, a squeeze of lemon juice, the cayenne pepper, and the remaining hard-cooked egg yolks, and pulse the blender for 4–5 seconds. Pour this mixture into a mixing bowl and add the chopped cornichons and chives. Fold all the ingredients together and chill the sauce.

Make the blinis: mix the yeast with the water and leave for 5 minutes until frothy. Put the yeast mix, milk, flour, egg yolks, salt, sugar, and melted butter in a blender and whizz for 40 seconds. Switch off, scrape the mixture down the sides and whizz again for a few seconds. Pour the batter into a large bowl and cover loosely. Leave to rise in a warm place for 1½–2 hours.

Beat the egg whites until stiff and fold into the batter. Heat a griddle or heavy skillet, brush with butter and drop teaspoonfuls of the batter on the pan or griddle. When bubbles start to appear on the surface, turn the blinis over and cook for a few minutes longer. They should be lightly browned on both sides. Keep the blinis warm while making the rest.

Make the salmon tartare: cut the salmon fillet into long thin slices, cut the slices again until you have long thin strips, then cut these across into small cubes. Place the salmon cubes in a mixing bowl with a good pinch of salt and the olive oil, and mix together. Then mix in the sauce gribiche.

Gently shred the reserved hard-cooked egg whites. Using a teaspoon, spoon a small dollop of the salmon tartare on each blini, garnish each with a little finely shredded egg white, followed by a pinch of caviar, a sprinkling of chives, and a dusting of cayenne or black pepper.

8 ounces salmon fillet

a good pinch of salt

1 tablespoon olive oil

¾ ounce (1½ tablespoons) lumpfish roe, Avruga (Spanish herring caviar) or salmon eggs and chopped chives, to garnish

for the sauce gribiche

4 eggs, hard-cooked and shelled, plus 2 extra raw egg yolks

1 shallot, quartered

1 garlic clove

1 teaspoon red or white wine vinegar

4 fl. oz. (½ cup) olive oil

1 teaspoon mustard

juice of 1 lemon

a pinch of cayenne pepper

3 cornichons (gherkins), finely chopped

a small bunch of chives, finely chopped

cayenne or black pepper, to finish

for the blinis

¾ ounce of dried yeast

4 fl. oz. (½ cup) warm water

8 fluid ounces (1 cup) milk

8 ounces (2 cups) all-purpose flour

3 eggs, separated

½ teaspoon salt

a pinch of sugar

2½ ounces melted butter, plus more for the skillet

Makes about 32

broiled chicken skewers
with salsa dragoncella

First make the salsa dragoncella: using a cheese shredder, gently shred the hard-cooked eggs into a mixing bowl. Stir in the tarragon, capers, mustard, and garlic. Now add the olive oil and red wine vinegar with salt and pepper to taste, and mix well. Place to one side or chill in the refrigerator.

Butterfly each chicken breast by cutting through the middle of the chicken horizontally as if you were cutting open a bap. Then cut each of the halves lengthwise into 4 strips. Place the chicken in a large mixing bowl. Mix the dried herbs and spices with the pepper and oil, throw this mixture into the bowl and make sure all the chicken is well coated.

Preheat a hot broiler. Thread the meat lengthwise on 16 skewers, preferably wooden, so you have long pieces of meat on your skewers like chicken satay, leaving enough room at one end of the skewer for you to hold. Lay some aluminum foil over your broiler pan, place the skewered chicken on the foil and drizzle lightly with olive oil. Cook under the hot broiler for 4–5 minutes, turn over and broil for a further 3–4 minutes.

Serve on a large dish with the long end of the skewer facing outwards. Spoon over the salsa and finish with a twist of pepper.

4 chicken breasts

1 tablespoon dried oregano

1 tablespoon garlic salt

1 tablespoon celery salt

1 tablespoon ground cumin

a good pinch of white pepper

2 tablespoons olive oil, plus more for drizzling

for the salsa dragoncella

3 hard-cooked eggs, shelled

a bunch of fresh tarragon, finely chopped

1 teaspoon capers, drained and finely chopped

1 tablespoon Dijon mustard

1 garlic clove, finely chopped

3 tablespoons olive oil

4 teaspoons red wine vinegar

salt and pepper

Makes 16 skewers

roast oriental marinated chicken wings

In my experience of party food, there should be a mixture of hot and cold food. This dish is best marinated overnight and then cooked thoroughly before your guests arrive. These lovely nibbles are very popular, so make loads.

The day before: place all the chicken wings in a large bowl. Give the dressing a really good shake and pour two-thirds of it over the chicken. Cover and leave to marinate in the refridgerator overnight.

Next day: preheat the oven to 350°F. Give your chicken wings a good mix up and place them in a single layer on a baking sheet (you may need to use a couple of baking sheets). Sprinkle with the sesame seeds and cook for 30–40 minutes, turning them halfway through. (Ovens do vary, so check and turn after 15 minutes; when sufficiently cooked the meat should pull away from the bone very easily, leaving the bone clean.) Serve piled high on a plate with wedges of lime and garnished with cilantro leaves.

2 pounds chicken wings (about 40)

1 pint (2½ cups) Oriental Teriyaki Dressing (2 recipe quantities, page 45)

2 tablespoons sesame seeds

handful of cilantro, for garnish

5 limes, to serve

Makes about 40

Keep your herb stalks in a jar for stocks and sauces, or to use as skewers.

It is getting as much air in your batter as possible that will make your Yorkies rise!

It is important to add the Yorkshire pudding mix to hot oil as this seals the puddings immediately and stops them sticking to the metal of the tray.

seared sliced beef
with miniature yorkshire puddings, arugula & horseradish dressing

First make the dressing: in a blender, blitz the garlic for 1 minute, then add the arugula and mustard, and pulse for no more than 5 seconds. Add the horseradish, lemon juice and olive oil. Season to taste and chill. This will keep for 2–3 days in the refrigerator.

Preheat the oven to 425°F. Put the olive oil in a small roasting pan and place it in the oven. Trim the beef fillet of all fat and sinew, and lightly season with salt and pepper. Strip the thyme leaves from the stalks and finely chop the leaves. Remove the roasting pan from the oven and place over a moderate heat on the stove. Place the beef fillet in the pan and seal on all sides until nut-brown. Sprinkle with the chopped thyme leaves, put the fillet in the pan in the oven and cook for a further 5 minutes. Remove, leaving the oven on, and pour the balsamic vinegar over the beef. Move the fillet around in the balsamic juices as they caramelize. Now place to one side and allow to cool.

3 tablespoons olive oil

2 pounds beef fillet

a bunch of fresh thyme

a splash of balsamic vinegar

for the arugula & horseradish dressing

2 garlic cloves

a bunch of arugula (about 2 ounces)

1 teaspoon Dijon mustard

1 tablespoon horseradish sauce

juice of 1 lemon

9 fluid ounces (1 cup) olive oil

salt and pepper

for the Yorkshire puddings

4 eggs

4 ounces (1 cup) self-rising flour

½ pint (2½ cups) milk

a good pinch of salt

4 tablespoons olive oil

Makes 12 puddings

Make the Yorkshire puddings: whisk the eggs in a blender until light and fluffy, about 4 minutes. Sift the flour on to a sheet of paper and then slowly, by lifting the sides of the paper, funnel it into the blender. Blend in the flour and then slowly add the milk, followed by a good pinch of salt.

Pour a teaspoon of oil into the bottom of each of the indentations on a small 12-hole tartlet pan (or muffin pan) and heat the pan in the oven for 3 minutes. Remove the pan carefully and pour the batter to the brim of each recess. Place the filled pan back in the oven and cook for about 20 minutes, until the Yorkshires are risen but not quite golden brown. Remove the Yorkshires from the oven.

Slice the beef as thinly as you can and curl a slice of meat in the center of each Yorkshire, flash back in the oven for a couple of minutes and remove. Place the Yorkshires on a large plate and spoon over the arugula and horseradish dressing. Once you get going with this recipe, you can create a veritable production line.

trimmed lamb cutlets
with salsa verde & olives

Generally, lamb chops are sold from the butchers in racks of about 6 cutlets. You can ask your butcher to cut them – you want your racks cut into cutlets with all the fat trimmed off. Alternatively, if you're going to cook a lot of cutlets, pre-order the number you'd like.

First make the salsa verde: finely chop together the garlic, anchovies and capers, place in a large bowl and mix together to a paste. Add the chopped mint and parsley, mustard, and vinegar. Stir together and, as you stir, slowly add the olive oil. Once this is all mixed in, season and chill. Turn your broiler on to full.

Slice the olives, put them in a bowl and mix in the rosemary, lemon juice, a touch of oil, and salt and pepper.

Place the chops on the oven pan (you should get approximately 10 cutlets on at once) and brush them with olive oil. Broil the chops for about 3 minutes on each side.

Remove and place on a large warmed dish with the bone facing outwards like a handle. Dress all the chops with the olives, followed by the salsa verde.

24 lamb cutlets
olive oil, for brushing
rosemary sprigs and
lemon slices, to garnish
(optional)

for the salsa verde

1 garlic clove
5 anchovy fillets
1 teaspoon capers
a bunch of mint, finely chopped
a bunch of flat-leaf parsley, finely chopped
1 teaspoon Dijon mustard
1 tablespoon red wine vinegar
6 tablespoons olive oil
salt and pepper

for the olives

7 ounces (2 cups) pitted olives
a bunch of rosemary
juice of 1 lemon
a little olive oil

Makes 24

miniature sausages
with chile & marmalade glaze

The idea for this recipe came from when we were kids at school, eating sausages at breakfast. Ketchup not being on the menu, we experimented with marmalade and discovered to our delight that it didn't taste at all bad. Recipe perfected, the marmalade marinade gives a delicious spicy-sweet flavor that complements the chipolatas. Blanching the chipolatas or any sausage first, before broiling, helps them cook better and taste better, as the blanching breaks down the fat. Try it, it really makes a difference.

24 chipolatas
1¾ ounces (1½ tablespoons) smooth marmalade
1 red chile, seeded and finely chopped
1 garlic clove, sliced
1 teaspoon ground allspice

Makes 24

Preheat the oven to 350°F. Bring a large saucepan of water to a boil, drop your chipolatas into the boiling water and immediately pull from the heat. When the water has cooled to lukewarm, the chipolatas will be perfectly blanched and ready to cook.

While the sausages are cooling, make your glaze. In a large saucepan, mix the marmalade, chile, garlic, and allspice with 3 tablespoons of water. Cook over a low heat, gently pushing the marmalade with the back of a fork to help break it down.

Once your mixture has become smooth, take your sausages out of the water, pat dry and lay out in an oven dish. Spoon a little of the chile marmalade over each sausage, place in the oven and cook for 20 minutes. After each 5 minutes of cooking, give the oven dish a little shake, to make sure the sausages are well coated in the glaze. Serve with or without cocktail sticks, no ketchup necessary.

This goes well with a chopped cherry tomato and basil salad.

An alternative base for this mixture is to make crostini toast; see the recipe overleaf.

ham on toast
with celery root, emmenthal, & green olives

This delicious party snack is simple to put together and makes a lovely twist on the usual ham on toast.

12 ounces Emmenthal cheese, shredded

¼ celery root, shredded

16 slices of good ham, cut into thin slivers

4 ounces (1 cup) pitted green olives, chopped

2 egg yolks

3 tablespoons olive oil, plus more for drizzling

juice of ½ lemon

1 garlic clove, finely chopped

a pinch of dried or chopped fresh oregano

salt and pepper

8 slices of good bread

Serves 8

Mix the cheese and celery root together in a bowl, then add the ham, olives, and the egg yolks and mix together. Stir in the olive oil, lemon juice, garlic, oregano, salt and pepper, and mix well. Preheat a hot broiler.

Drizzle the slices of bread lightly with olive oil, and toast lightly on both sides. Spread the mixture on one side of the bread, whack under the broiler and toast again until golden brown.

Cut each slice of toast into 4 pieces and serve.

For a nice tang to these crostini, use a mustard vinaigrette to dress the leeks.

prosciutto crostini

with quail's egg, cherry tomatoes, & poached leeks

Preheat the oven to 325°F. Cover a baking sheet with a cooling rack. Slice the baguette thinly at an angle to get 24 large slices.

Put the butter, garlic, peppercorns, and herbs in a saucepan and melt the butter over the lowest possible heat until it has separated. Brush the clarified butter over the slices of bread.

Once the oven is hot, bake the bread until golden, about 5 minutes, and remove, then allow to cool.

Bring 2 saucepans of salted water to a boil. When the water is boiling vigorously, carefully add the quails' eggs to one and boil for exactly 2½ minutes. Immediately drain and tip the eggs into iced water. Once they are cool, carefully shell and cut in half.

Add the leeks to the other pan of boiling water, turn the heat down and allow the leeks to cook slowly for 10 minutes. Drain and put on a plate. Drizzle with olive oil or vinaigrette while still warm and leave to cool.

Cut the prosciutto slices in half lengthwise. Using the handle of a teaspoon, place a small dollop of crème fraîche on the center of each crostini. Now add a strip of prosciutto, arranging it around the bread and using the crème fraîche to hold it in place. Add a little more crème fraîche to the prosciutto, place half a quail's egg in the center together with half a cherry tomato. Take a leek and cut it into 3 inch pieces lengthwise. Place a piece of leek on top of the egg and cherry tomato. Drizzle each crostini with a little more olive oil and a twist of black pepper, and serve.

1 long fresh baguette

8 ounces (2 sticks) butter, melted

2 garlic cloves

a good pinch of black peppercorns

a sprig of fresh thyme

a sprig of fresh rosemary

salt

12 quails' eggs, halved

iced water

6 baby leeks

a little olive oil or vinaigrette

12 slices of prosciutto

3 tablespoons crème fraîche

12 cherry tomatoes, halved

Makes 24

Toffee- and Chocolate-
dipped Fruits, served
around the world as
petits fours, make a
relatively simple finale
for your party food.

toffee-dipped fruits

These are based on the same principle as toffee apples, and the type of
toffee you will need to make is called 'hard crack'. You can test for hard
crack by taking a drop of your boiling sugar syrup in a spoon and placing
the spoon directly into ice-cold water. The toffee should immediately
become solid.

First prepare the fruits by peeling the mandarins and dividing them into segments
(start with these so, once peeled, the skins of the segments have time to become
papery and dry); place to one side. Gently wash the gooseberries and strawberries
and pat dry – do not remove any stalks or leaves.

Lightly grease a wire cooling rack (like the rack in your broiler) and place it on
top of some paper towel. Make sure your fruit is at hand, ready to dip. Put the sugar
in a saucepan with 2 tablespoons water and heat gently, stirring until the sugar has
dissolved in the water. Then increase the heat to moderate and slowly bring the
sugar mixture to a boil. The mixture will start to color and smoke slightly, but do not
worry, it's part of the process. Once your mixture is toffee-colored and at the hard-
crack stage (see above), which takes about 5 minutes, turn the heat off.

Start with the strawberries, as the longer they are left out the softer they
become. Carefully holding the stem of each strawberry, dip about two-thirds of the
fruit into the toffee, then place on the cooling rack. Then dip the gooseberries,
holding the leaves, and finally dip half of each mandarin segment. Once all the fruits
are dipped, place them to one side to cool and start on your chocolate-dipped fruits.

2 mandarins

24 cape gooseberries

a container of
strawberries

vegetable oil, for greasing

6 ounces (¾ cup)
granulated sugar

Serves 8

chocolate-dipped fruits

The ingredients are exactly the same as for the toffee-dipped fruits, but instead of sugar syrup we use chocolate, which is melted gently in a bain-marie or bowl set over a pan of gently simmering water. Don't allow it to melt too quickly as this can cause the chocolate to split.

While this is melting, lay out 1 or 2 large sheets of waxed paper in baking sheets. Dip the strawberries and gooseberries as opposite, allowing excess chocolate to drip off and placing on the paper. Then do the same with the cooled toffee-coated mandarin segments, dipping the other ends into the chocolate. Place them on the waxed paper and allow all the chocolate fruits to set (you may need to place the sheets in the fridge). Once set, dust the chocolate fruits with confectioners' sugar.

6 ounces good-quality semi-sweet chocolate

a container of strawberries

24 cape gooseberries

2 mandarins, separated into segments and dipped in toffee as above

confectioners' sugar, to dust

Serves 8

iced peaches in champagne

16 peaches

bottles of sparkling wine or Champagne

½ pint (1¼ cups) cream, freshly whipped

sugar to taste

Serves 8

I first heard of this recipe from our wine supplier, Berard, who was invited to a garden party by one of the famous champagne houses. His hosts had filled a large fountain with their latest vintage and into that had then tipped hundreds of peaches, which spun wildly in the champagne, infusing it with peach flavor. The peaches spin because they are each pierced with a fork and then frozen. As the fruit begins to thaw, the bubbles enter the holes made by the fork and push the peaches into a spin. You will need one or two large punch bowls or very large salad bowls. The peaches must float and be able to move.

At least 4 hours ahead, prepare the peaches: using a fork, gently pierce the flesh of each peach all the way to the stone, following the curve of the fork. Remove the fork, again carefully following the curve of the holes you have just made. Move the fork 2 inches around the fruit and make another set of holes. Keep going until you have a band of holes around the peach, then immediately freeze for at least 4 hours.

When you are ready to serve your champagne, fill the bowls with champagne and immediately add the peaches. As they thaw, they will start to spin. Once the champagne is finished, take the peaches and serve them individually or all together in a bowl, with freshly whipped cream and a sprinkling of sugar.

pimm's & peach water ice

Put the sugar, Pimm's, and lemonade into a small saucepan, heat gently until the sugar is dissolved, then boil for 3 minutes. Pull from the heat and leave until cool. Bring a large saucepan of water to a boil and blanch the peaches for 1 minute only. Remove, allow to cool and remove the skins and pits. Immediately purée the peach pulp in a blender or through a strainer. Add the lemon juice and cold syrup to the purée and pour the mixture into a shallow dish suitable for freezing. Place in the freezer for 15 minutes until semi-frozen. Pour back into a bowl and whisk vigorously for a couple of minutes, return to the tray and freeze until firm.

Transfer to the refrigerator about 20 minutes before serving, to allow the sorbet to soften a little. To serve, scoop into individual glasses, garnish with a slice of cucumber and a sprig of mint.

4 ounces (½ cup) superfine sugar

3 tablespoons Pimm's

3½ fluid ounces (⅓ cup) lemonade

4 large peaches

juice of 1 lemon

cucumber slices and mint sprigs, to decorate

Serves 8

sparkling fruit cocktails

a container of strawberries, raspberries or blackberries (or use your imagination, but berries do work very well)

juice of ½ lemon

1 teaspoon granulated sugar

1 ice cube

2 bottles of sparkling wine or champagne

Serves 10
(5 glasses per bottle)

Based on the same idea as the Bellini, which is made from peach juice and champagne, these are easy to prepare and wonderful served at parties, especially in the summer, outdoors at barbecues.

First blend the fruit, lemon juice, and sugar with the ice cube until you have a purée. Pour about ½ inch of purée into each champagne flute, then slowly pour in the champagne and gently stir. Serve immediately.

Everybody loves a picnic, especially children, and they are guaranteed to bring out the child in you too. If I'm ever having problems with my son saying 'I'm not hungry', I announce that lunch will be a picnic, even if it's on the sitting room floor, and he magically gets his appetite back immediately.

Once you've made all your food and set off on your picnic, it is a good thing to remind yourself that you are carrying food and not to march off for hours in the sunshine before eating, to avoid eating warm sandwiches that could even become hazardous — so picnic first, walk afterwards.

picnics

pressed french bread
with ratatouille

This is a lovely simple recipe originally from Provence. It is best to cook ratatouille in a large-based casserole pot or deep skillet.

First make the ratatouille: heat the olive oil in a large saucepan, stir in the garlic and onions, and soften over a moderate heat. When soft, add the mixed peppers and turn the heat up to moderate-to-hot. Cook for a couple of minutes, then add the zucchini and eggplant. Cook for a further 2–3 minutes, stirring gently. Add the plum tomatoes and cook for a further 2 minutes, then reduce the heat to low and leave to simmer gently for 30 minutes, stirring every 5 minutes or so. Remove from the heat and add a good pinch of salt, a couple of twists of black pepper, and the chopped fresh herbs.

Slice the baguettes with one horizontal cut all the way through so you have 4 long halves. Using your fingers, scoop out the insides of the bread to make 4 'canoes'. Fill one half of each stick with ratatouille, place the other half on top and roll up separately in waxed paper or plastic wrap and tie each end up with string or sticky tape so it looks like a cracker, then tie an extra piece of string or tape around the middle of each to hold the filling in. Place a tray on the top of the baguettes and put a weight on the top (you can use a number of things for this, from cookbooks to serving plates). Place the weighted baguettes in the refridgerator and allow to firm for at least 2 hours. Unwrap and slice to eat.

2 large baguettes

for the ratatouille

6 tablespoons extra-virgin olive oil

1 garlic clove, finely chopped

1 onion, finely chopped

2 red bell peppers, seeded and chopped

1 yellow bell pepper, seeded and chopped

1 green bell pepper, seeded and chopped

4 zucchini, cut into small cubes

2 eggplant, chopped

7 ounce can of plum tomatoes, drained

salt and pepper

a handful of roughly chopped fresh oregano and basil (or your preferred herbs)

Serves 8

zucchini stuffed
with pine nuts, mint, parsley, & lemon rind

Preheat the oven to 350°F. Place the whole zucchini on a baking sheet, drizzle with a couple of tablespoons of olive oil and 2 tablespoons of white wine. Cook in the oven for about 5 minutes to soften, remove and allow to cool.

Add the pine nuts to a saucepan with a little olive oil and cook for a couple of minutes on a low heat. Meanwhile, very carefully scoop out the insides of the zucchini (the best way to do this is to use an apple corer or a small teaspoon), cut the zucchini into 4 inch pieces and put the scooped-out flesh in the pan with the pine nuts. Still over a low heat, try to dry out as much of the moisture from the zucchini pulp as possible. After 5 minutes, pull the saucepan from the heat and allow the zucchini pulp to cool.

When cool, add the chopped parsley and mint, finely chopped onion and garlic, and the lemon rind. Stir well and, with the back of a fork, mash the ingredients together. Fold in the Parmesan cheese and season with salt and pepper.

Using a teaspoon, fill the hollowed-out zucchini with the stuffing and lay the stuffed zucchini on their sides back on the baking sheet. Drizzle with more olive oil and cook in the oven for 10–15 minutes.

Remove, allow to cool and then chill for at least 2 hours. Once well chilled, pack into a container and take on your picnic.

8 large zucchini

about 6 tablespoons olive oil

2 tablespoons white wine

5 ounces (1½ cups) pine nuts

a bunch of fresh parsley, chopped

a bunch of fresh mint, chopped

1 red onion, finely chopped

1 garlic clove, finely chopped

finely shredded rind of 2 lemons

4 ounces (1½ cups) Parmesan cheese

salt and pepper

Serves 8

soft-cooked quails' eggs
in tomato olive oil

The most important thing in this recipe is to take your time when peeling the eggs.

First make the tomato olive oil: add the olive oil to a small saucepan with the cherry tomatoes and thyme, if you have it, and simmer gently for 30 minutes.

In a large saucepan, bring 2 pints (5 cups) of salted water to a vigorous boil. Add the quails' eggs, cover and cook for exactly 1 minute 15 seconds. Immediately drain and place the eggs straight into a bowl of iced water, placing the bowl of water in the sink under cold running water for a couple of minutes.

Remove the tomatoes and oil from heat. Using a fork, squish the tomatoes into the oil, then place back on the heat to simmer for a further 5 minutes. Strain the tomatoes into a bowl.

Take each quail's egg and gently tap the shell on the kitchen counter, then carefully shell. Lay the shelled eggs gently on a dish towel to absorb any moisture. Add the eggs to the cooled tomato oil, together with a twist of black pepper and a pinch of salt. Pour this into a large jar and pop in the refridgerator, where they will keep for up to 2 days.

When you're serving the eggs, use a spoon rather than a fork, as the insides of the eggs are still soft.

salt and pepper

24 quails' eggs

iced water

for the tomato olive oil

7 fluid ounces (¾ cup) olive oil

6 cherry tomatoes

a good sprig of fresh thyme (if available)

Serves 6–8

If you like, you can add a seeded and chopped red chile to the salsa for some authentic chili heat.

layered fajitas
with mixed salsa torte

While on my travels, I spent some time in Mexico. I don't think I could have had a more authentic experience as I stayed with a Mexican family for two months. One day out, we ended up at a rodeo, where this style of fajita was being served to the crowds.

First make the fajitas: pour the flour and salt into a mixing bowl, make a well in the center and add ½ pint (1¼ cups) water. Mix together, adding a little more water, if necessary, until you have a firm dough. Knead the dough until nice and smooth, then cut into 6 pieces and shape into balls. Roll each ball out to a 7 inch round.

Heat a teaspoon of corn oil in a skillet and cook each fajita on both sides until it puffs up and immediately remove from the heat.

Make the filling: if using soaked dried beans, drain them, add to a saucepan of boiling water and cook gently for 2 hours; if using canned beans, drain and add to a saucepan with ½ pint (1¼ cups) water and cook gently for 30 minutes.

Add 4 tablespoons of the corn oil to a saucepan and cook the onion, chile and garlic until softened. Add the drained beans and cook for a further 10 minutes, stirring, then start to mash the beans roughly with the back of a fork, adding a little more corn oil, the chopped cilantro, a dash of Tabasco, and the lime juice. Stir well and pull from heat.

Make the salsa by mixing together all the ingredients.

Lay each fajita on a plate, spoon over a quarter of the bean filling, add a dollop of sour cream, drizzle with a little salsa and repeat layering your 5 fajitas until you come to the final fajita which you use as a lid, pressing down firmly. Top with the remaining salsa, place in the refridgerator and allow to set. Cut into pie wedges and eat outdoors.

for the fajitas

6 ounces (1½ cups) all-purpose flour

a good pinch of salt

corn oil, for frying

for the filling

2 x 14 ounce cans of red beans (or 7 ounces (1 cup) dried beans soaked for 24 hours)

6 tablespoons corn oil

1 onion, chopped

1 red chile, seeded and chopped

1 garlic clove, chopped

½ bunch of fresh cilantro, chopped

a dash of Tabasco sauce

juice of 1 lime

9 fluid ounces (1 cup) sour cream

for the salsa

4 tomatoes, seeded and chopped

½ bunch of fresh cilantro (stalks and all), chopped

½ red onion, chopped

3 tablespoons corn oil

cod & parsley flan
with sun-dried tomatoes

In this traditional English flan, it is important to use good fresh cod or any other flaky white fish, though you could even use smoked haddock.

First make the pastry: sift the flour and salt into a bowl, then rub in the chopped softened butter, followed by the egg yolk and the iced water. Knead lightly until smooth. Chill the pastry while you make the filling. Preheat the oven to 400°F.

Poach the cod: place the cod fillets in a saucepan, add the bay leaf, a twist of black pepper, and the mustard. Pour over the milk, bring just to a boil and simmer gently for 3 minutes. Remove from the heat and leave to cool to room temperature.

Make the filling: in a bowl, whisk the egg yolks and whole egg until well beaten. Add the cream, cheese, salt and pepper, and a dash of Worcestershire sauce. Now flake in the cod and gently stir in the cooled milk, followed by the parsley and sun-dried tomatoes. Allow to cool and then chill for 30 minutes.

Roll out the pastry and use to line a 12 inch flan ring. Prick the base of the pastry case with a fork. Line the pastry case with baking paper, cover with baking beans or dried beans and bake blind in the preheated oven for 15 minutes. Remove the beans and paper and return to the oven for a further 5 minutes to finish cooking the base. Reduce the oven setting to 350°F.

Allow the pastry case to cool a little, then pour in the filling and bake in the oven for about 30 minutes, until risen and golden brown.

for the pastry

8 ounces (2 cups) all-purpose flour

a pinch of salt

4 ounces (1 stick) butter

1 egg yolk

3 tablespoons iced water

for the cod

4 cod fillets, each about 6 ounces, skinned and any bones removed

1 bay leaf

pepper

1 teaspoon English mustard

1 pint (2½ cups) milk

for the filling

4 egg yolks, plus 1 whole egg

4 fluid ounces (½ cup) heavy cream

4 ounces (1½ cups) mature Cheddar cheese, shredded

a dash of Worcestershire sauce

a bunch of fresh parsley, finely chopped

2 ounces sun-dried tomatoes, drained, patted dry and finely chopped

Using the recipe opposite, you could also make 5 small flans, if you prefer, using 3 inch rings.

smoked trout & horseradish pâté

This pâté is wonderful served either in sandwiches or spread on crackers with sliced tomato and black pepper.

4 smoked trout fillets, skinned

2 teaspoons horseradish sauce

¼ pint (⅔ cup) heavy cream, whipped to soft peaks

a handful of chopped parsley

finely shredded rind of 1 lemon

1 shallot, finely chopped

salt and pepper

vegetable oil, for greasing

Makes 12 good slices

Flake the trout fillets into a bowl and add the horseradish, then fold in the whipped cream, parsley, lemon rind, shallot, salt and pepper, and mix well.

Lightly brush a medium terrine mold with oil and spoon in the pâté mixture, then press it down firmly. Chill for 2 hours before serving.

To serve, gently warm the terrine mold in warm water to make it easy to turn the pâté out. Cut it into thick slices.

Try orange gremolata
with game birds, or
even beef and pork.

Make a lemon or lime
gremolata for meaty fish,
like sea bass and tuna.

roast chicken drumsticks & thighs
with orange gremolata

First marinate the chicken: strip the thyme leaves from the thyme stalks, finely chop the thyme leaves and place the leaves in a bowl and the stalks in a deep-sided roasting pan. Shred the rind of the oranges and add to the bowl with the thyme leaves.

Squeeze the orange juice through a strainer into a separate bowl. Add to this the lime juice, Tabasco, and garlic. Using a sharp knife, cut deep scores into the chicken down to the bone, 2 to 3 times on each piece. Place the chicken in the orange juice marinade and allow to marinate for at least an hour.

Preheat the oven to 375°F. Remove the chicken from the marinade, place on top of the thyme stalks, drizzle with olive oil and sprinkle over the orange rind and chopped thyme leaves. Season well and cook in the oven for 15 minutes, then turn the oven down to 325°F and cook for a further 30 minutes. Remove.

4 chicken drumsticks and
4 thighs

a bunch of fresh thyme

2 oranges

juice of 1 lime

1 teaspoon Tabasco sauce

2 garlic cloves, sliced

a little olive oil

salt and pepper

Serves 8

small scotch eggs

The only difference here is that we are using quails' eggs instead of
hens' eggs.

Squeeze all the sausage meat out of the skins into a bowl and add 1 level tablespoon
flour, 1 of the eggs, the sage, garlic, lemon rind and juice, 1 heaped tablespoon of
the breadcrumbs, and a pinch of paprika. Mix all these ingredients together
thoroughly.

Shape the mixture into 12 balls, then place each ball between 2 sheets of plastic
wrap and press the ball to form a pattie (like a burger) about 3 inches in diameter.
Remove the top layer of plastic wrap and place a quail's eggs in the center of the
pattie, then take the bottom sheet of plastic wrap and bring it up around the egg, and
shape the sausage meat around the egg. Once you have a ball, remove the plastic
wrap and repeat with the other patties and eggs.

Beat the remaining eggs and put in a shallow plate; sprinkle the remaining flour
on to another plate and put the breadcrumbs on a third. Roll each ball first in the
flour, dip them in the egg and finally roll through the breadcrumbs.

In a deep-sided skillet or saucepan, fry the small scotch eggs in about 1 inch of
vegetable oil, 3 to 4 at a time, until golden brown, about 8 minutes. Remove carefully
using a slotted spoon and place on paper towel to drain. Allow to cool.

6 sausages

2 ounces (½ cup) all-purpose
flour

3 eggs

5 fresh sage leaves,
chopped, or 1 teaspoon
dried sage

1 garlic clove, finely
chopped

finely shredded rind of 1 lemon
and juice of ½ lemon

2 ounces (5 tablespoons)
breadcrumbs

a pinch of ground paprika

12 quails' eggs, hard-cooked
and shelled (see page 198)

vegetable oil, for frying

Makes 12

whole roast quail
stuffed with thyme, garlic, & lemon

This is a lovely alternative to chicken drumsticks. Quails have very little fat, so it's a good idea to add a stuffing to keep the meat tender, especially if you are going to cook and chill them for a picnic.

Preheat the oven to 350°F. Make the stuffing: squeeze the sausage meat out of the skins and place in a bowl. Mix in the lemon rind, chopped thyme leaves, mashed garlic, and olive oil. Blend all the stuffing ingredients together well, roll the mixture into 6 equally sized sausage shapes and stuff each quail with one.

Blend together the mustard and olive oil, and brush this mixture over the skin of each quail. Place the quails in a roasting pan and cook for 25–30 minutes. Remove and allow to cool.

These quails serve wonderfully well with redcurrant jelly.

6 quails

2 tablespoons Dijon mustard

3 teaspoons olive oil

redcurrant jelly, to serve (optional)

for the stuffing

3 large pork sausages

finely shredded rind of 2 lemons

a bunch of fresh thyme, leaves stripped from the stalks

1 garlic clove, mashed with a pinch of salt

5 teaspoons olive oil

Serves 6

cotechino sausage roll

Cotechino sausages are a type of fresh Italian sausage similar to zampone and slightly stronger in taste. They are usually cooked by boiling them in a bag filled with oil and then eaten with lentils and salsa verde. This recipe uses the meat from the cotechino sausage with some extra ingredients, all cooked in puff pastry.

Preheat the oven to 400°F and grease a baking sheet. Take the meat from the cotechino sausage and mix with all the other ingredients except the pastry and egg.

Cut the puff pastry into quarters and then into eighths. Roll each of these pieces into a strip 10 inches long and 3 inches wide. Place a thin strip of sausage meat one-third of the way in along the length of each pastry strip. Whisk the egg in a bowl and brush the egg wash around the sausage meat. Fold the pastry over the meat and seal all the edges by pressing down with your fingers. Cut the roll into 3 pieces and place on the prepared baking sheet.

Cook in the oven for 5 minutes, then turn the oven down to 325°F and cook for a further 10–12 minutes. Remove from the oven and allow to cool.

1 cotechino sausage

½ bunch of fresh mint, chopped

½ bunch of fresh parsley, chopped

2 garlic cloves, chopped

1 teaspoon capers, chopped

2 teaspoons Dijon mustard

1 teaspoon white wine vinegar

3 anchovies, chopped

pepper

8 ounces of ready-rolled puff pastry

1 egg

Makes about 24

When draining cooked vegetables, run cold water over them (refresh) or toss them in olive oil to stop them from browning.

fresh tuna niçoise

The wonderful thing about niçoise is that it is a satisfying meal in a salad. I've kept this dish as simple as possible, without the addition of salad leaves but using artichokes. Due to the weight of the other salad ingredients, salad leaves become bruised and soggy; if you do want to serve them with this dish, they are best served on the side.

10 new potatoes

a good handful of fine green beans

6 eggs

4 slices of fresh tuna, each about 2 ounces

a little olive oil

18 cherry tomatoes

½ cucumber

14 ounces canned artichoke hearts (or you could use fresh, prepared as described on page 36)

1 red onion

salt and pepper

3 tablespoons French Dressing (page 252) or Traditional Salad Dressing (page 250)

a small bunch of chives

4 ounces (1 cup) pitted black and green olives

8 anchovy fillets

Bring 3 saucepans of salted water to a boil. Boil the potatoes in one pan until tender, and drain. As the potatoes cook, blanch the beans for a couple of minutes, and refresh immediately in cold water. In the third pan, boil the eggs for 6 minutes, then place them straight into ice-cold water.

Heat a griddle pan or skillet to full heat, brush the tuna slices with a little olive oil and seal them on both sides. Remove and place on a plate to one side.

Start preparing the salad ingredients and adding them to a large mixing bowl: the cherry tomatoes, cut into halves, the cucumber cut into cubes, the green beans, the potatoes cut into ½ inch thick slices, the artichokes cut into quarters and half of the thinly sliced red onion. Mix gently, adding a pinch of salt and the dressing.

Plate up either individually or in one large serving dish, garnish around the edges with the shelled eggs cut lengthwise into halves. Place the tuna slices on top, sprinkle over the finely chopped chives, olives, and anchovy fillets. Chill well before serving.

Just before serving, add a light squeeze of lemon juice and a couple of twists of black pepper.

My favorite way of eating ham is to slice it thinly, laying the slices of ham over fresh ciabatta bread which has been drizzled with virgin olive oil, then placing some slices of tomato over the top, followed by a twist of black pepper. Then I spread it with either homemade Piccalilli (page 233) or Pear and Apple Chutney (page 235). Alternatively, if it's chucking it down with rain, this makes a great toasted sandwich.

homemade ham
with mustard, sugar, & garlic glaze

It's a very satisfying thing, making your own ham. It's also inexpensive compared to bought ham, so I wonder why so much is charged for something that is so simple to make. Recently I discovered a new way of preparing ham, infusing it with truffles throughout, giving it such an exquisite taste that my mouth is watering at the thought.

1 head of garlic
1 teaspoon black peppercorns
1 tablespoon vinegar
2–3 parsley stalks
2 pound piece of raw ham
4 tablespoons brown sugar
a good pinch of salt
2 tablespoons English mustard

Serves 8

First prepare the poaching liquor: half-fill a large deep saucepan with water, cut the garlic head in half horizontally and add this together with the peppercorns, vinegar and parsley stalks. Bring to a boil, add the ham, turn the heat down and gently poach the meat for 80 minutes. Remove from the heat and allow to cool.

Remove the ham from the cooled liquor, put it in the refrigerator and let it chill for 1 hour at least.

Meanwhile, remove 8 fluid ounces (1 cup) of the poaching liquor from the pan and pour it into a saucepan, together with the boiled garlic cloves. Add the sugar, a pinch of salt and the mustard. Combine these ingredients together, mashing the peeled garlic with the back of a fork until you have a purée. Bring the purée to a boil and gently reduce it by half (about 20 minutes). Remove from the heat and allow to cool.

Take the ham out of the refrigerator, brush the cooled purée all over it and put it back in the refridgerator for about 10 minutes. Repeat this process until you have built up a good layer of glaze on the ham.

You can vary the beans in this salad according to what's available: try red kidney beans, cannellini beans or even chickpeas.

mixed bean salad
with rice

Adding the beans and rice to the dressing while they're still warm really infuses the dressing flavors into them and their heat also gently cooks the spinach.

Bring a large saucepan of salted water to a boil, add the rice and bring back to a boil. Cover and simmer for 10 minutes. Drain and place to one side.

While the rice is cooking, make the dressing by whisking all the ingredients together well in a bowl.

Add the green beans and peas to another saucepan of boiling salted water and boil for 2 minutes. Add the drained canned navy beans and boil for a further minute, then drain.

Immediately add the warm beans and peas to the dressing and stir in well. Then stir in the rice thoroughly, adding a pinch of salt and a couple of twists of pepper.

salt and pepper

9 ounces (1½ cups) rice
(long-grain or basmati)

4 ounces French green
beans, halved

4 ounces frozen peas

9 ounce can of
navy beans, drained

for the dressing

1 bag of spinach, finely
chopped

1 garlic clove, finely
chopped

1 level teaspoon dried
oregano

1 teaspoon ground
coriander

1 level teaspoon ground
cumin

2 tablespoons lemon juice

4 fluid ounces (½ cup) good
olive oil

Serves 8

potato, egg, red onion, & tarragon salad

First make the dressing: in a large mixing bowl, mix the chopped peppers, garlic, red onion, vinegar, and a good pinch of salt. Place this to one side.

Boil the eggs for 10 minutes. Drain and leave under cold running water for a couple of minutes.

At the same time as the eggs are cooking, boil the potato cubes until just soft, 7–10 minutes, then drain.

Add the olive oil to the dressing and immediately add the hot potatoes, followed by the chopped tarragon leaves.

Shell the boiled eggs and then shred them into the salad. Season and, using a large spoon, gently fold all the ingredients together.

4 eggs

4 large potatoes, cut into small cubes

a good pinch of cayenne pepper, to garnish

for the dressing

2 red bell peppers, seeded and finely chopped

1 garlic clove, crushed

1 red onion, thinly sliced

1 tablespoon white wine vinegar

salt

10 fluid ounces (1¼ cups) olive oil

a bunch of tarragon, leaves stripped from stalks and finely chopped

Serves 6–8

rolled crêpes
filled with spinach, ricotta cheese, & prosciutto

First make the filling: squeeze the cooked spinach in a clean dish towel to get it as dry as possible. Add to a bowl with the garlic, ricotta, mascarpone, olive oil, lemon juice, salt, pepper, and nutmeg. Stir together well.

Make the crêpes: mix together the eggs, flour, oil, and salt, and whisk well, making sure there are no lumps. Add the melted butter and slowly add the milk until you have a smooth pancake batter. Stir in the oregano.

Heat a little olive oil in a skillet and start to make about 24 large pancakes that are as thin as possible, tilting the pan to spread the batter thinly and cooking them for about 20 seconds on each side. As they are cooked, stack them on top of each other until all the batter is finished. Place them to one side.

Using a palette knife, spread the filling thinly over each pancake, then lay the thin slices of prosciutto over the filling. Roll each pancake up around the meat into cylinder shapes and whack them into the refridgerator for an hour or so.

Remove the crêpes from refridgerator and cut each cylinder across into 3 inch slices, place in a container and go.

2 eggs

8 ounces (2 cups) all-purpose flour

1 tablespoon olive oil, plus more for frying

a pinch of salt

2 ounces (½ stick) unsalted butter, melted

1 pint (2½ cups) milk

2 teaspoons dried oregano

for the filling

9 ounces cooked spinach

1 garlic clove, finely chopped

9 ounces (1¼ cups) ricott cheese

4 ounces mascarpone cheese

1 teaspoon olive oil

1 teaspoon lemon juice

a pinch of salt

a pinch of pepper

a pinch of freshly shredded nutmeg

8 slices of prosciutto, each cut into 3 lengthwise

Makes about 24

victoria sandwich
with assorted fillings

I first remember coming across this recipe at catering college and finding it fascinating that you could turn a loaf of sandwich bread into a savory gâteau. This was something I'd never seen before in my life, probably due to the fact that it has fallen out of fashion. Well, I figure it's long overdue a revival. You can pretty much put any fillings into this as long as they are pre-mixed with either cream cheese, ricotta, crème fraîche, or mayonnaise to ensure that the gâteau will stick together.

1 uncut sandwich loaf (traditionally you would trim off all the crusts, but I don't bother to do that)

suggested fillings:

chopped ham with mustard mayonnaise, capers, and parsley

prawns with Marie-Rose sauce

crab with horseradish mayonnaise

cream cheese with salted cucumber and chives

egg mayonnaise

Makes 12 portions

First prepare a chopping board by covering with plastic, leaving the plastic wrap attached to its roll, so that you can pull it all the way around the loaf once it is filled.

Place your loaf on another chopping board and make 4 horizontal cuts through the bread to create 5 large, long slices. Lay these slices down on the prepared board and spread your filling about ½ inch thick on the bottom slice of bread, then place the next slice on top and spread the filling again, continuing until you come to the top slice, which you don't put any filling on!

Once you've completed this you should have your loaf reassembled. Now bring the plastic wrap up around it, wrapping it securely. Place in the refridgerator to chill for at least an hour.

When it is set, unwrap the sandwich, take a sharp knife and slice as you would a normal loaf, keeping the slices about 1 inch thick. Push the slices back together to re-form a loaf, wrap in plastic wrap again and you're ready to go.

apricot tarts & almond tarts

I've used apricots as a filling, but you could replace them with any other seasonal soft fruit, like strawberries or blackcurrants and omit the cinnamon.

First make the pastry: sift the flour, confectioners' sugar, and salt into a large mixing bowl and mix together. Add the softened butter and, using your fingertips, rub it into the flour until you have a breadcrumb consistency. In a separate bowl, whisk the egg and orange rind together with 1 tablespoon of water. Add this to the flour mixture and stir, then work the mixture together until you have a dough. Wrap the dough in plastic wrap and place in the refridgerator to rest for at least 30 minutes.

Meanwhile, make the apricot filling: put the apricots in a saucepan and simmer until reduced to a thick purée. Pull from the heat and leave to cool. Mix together the butter, sugar, cinnamon, and a squeeze of lemon juice, then mix this all into the cooled apricot purée. Cover and chill until required.

Now, make the almond filling: whisk the egg white until stiff, then fold in the sugar, ground almonds, and Amaretto or rum. Cover and chill in the refridgerator until required.

Preheat the oven to 350°F and grease two 12-hole tartlet pans. Remove the pastry from the refridgerator, lightly flour a work surface and roll the pastry out to fill the 24 tartlet molds (if your indentations are 3 inches across, use a 4 inch cutter). Ease each round into a mold on the baking pan and prick the bases with a fork. Bake in the oven for 5 minutes.

Remove, allow to cool, spoon in the fillings and place back in the oven for a further 15 minutes. Remove and allow to cool.

for the sweet pastry

1 pound (4 cups) all-purpose flour

5 ounces (1½ cups) confectioners' sugar

a pinch of salt

8 ounces (2 sticks) unsalted butter, plus more for greasing

1 large egg

1 tablespoon shredded orange rind

for the apricot filling

14 ounces apricots, peeled, pitted and chopped

2 tablespoons unsalted butter

2 tablespoons superfine sugar

1 teaspoon of ground cinnamon

a squeeze of lemon juice

for the almond filling

white of 1 large or 2 small egg(s)

3 tablespoons granulated sugar

3 tablespoons ground almonds

1½ tablespoons Amaretto or light rum

Makes 24 (12 of each)

treacle tarts

Make and chill the pastry, then use to line 24 tartlet molds and bake blind as described above.

Make the molasses filling: in a saucepan, gently heat the golden syrup, stir in the lemon juice, lemon rind and breadcrumbs and pull from heat.

Spoon the filling into the cooled tartlet shells and place back in the oven for a further 15 minutes. Remove and allow to cool.

1 recipe quantity of sweet pastry (page 216)

for the molasses filling

8 tablespoons golden syrup

finely shredded rind and juice of 1 lemon

3 cups fresh breadcrumbs

Makes about 24

brownies

14 ounces plain dark chocolate

10 ounces (2½ sticks) unsalted butter, plus more for greasing

9 ounces (1¼ cups) superfine sugar

4 eggs

4 ounces (1 cup) all-purpose flour

1 teaspoon baking powder

Makes 12 pieces

Preheat the oven to 350°F and grease the insides of an 8 inch square baking pan, then line the base with baking paper.

Bring a saucepan one-third filled with water to a boil, then reduce the heat to a simmer. Break 6 ounces of the chocolate into a heatproof bowl, sit the bowl over the saucepan and allow the chocolate to melt. Chop the remaining chocolate into chunks and place to one side.

Once the chocolate in the bowl has melted, add the butter and stir until melted and blended. Pull from the heat and stir in the sugar. Beat the eggs, stir into the chocolate mixture and mix together well.

Sift the flour and baking powder into another mixing bowl and slowly fold in the chocolate mixture. Stir in the reserved chocolate chunks, then pour the mix into the baking pan and cook for 25–30 minutes until firm. Allow to cool a little, then turn out on a wire rack to cool fully. Slice into squares to serve.

nottingham nut cake

With no butter or flour, this great recipe I learnt in Nottingham really is quite unique, being extremely light in weight but dense in texture. Just about any combination of nuts will work, but these are my favorites.

9 ounces (1⅔ cups) shelled pistachios

9 ounces (1⅔ cups) blanched almonds

6 eggs, separated

3 tablespoons superfine sugar

1½ ounces dried apricots, chopped (optional)

2 drops of vanilla extract

Serves 8–10

Preheat the oven to 400°F. Line a 10 inch cake pan or medium-sized bread pan with baking paper, cutting an extra base shape to use to cover the cake with later.

Blitz the nuts in a blender or grind in a pestle and mortar. Whisk the egg yolks with 2 tablespoons of superfine sugar until slightly thick and fluffy. Then whisk the egg whites with the remaining sugar until thick and fluffy (shaving-foam consistency). Add the ground nuts to a large bowl together with the chopped apricots if you are using them, and the vanilla extract. Then gently fold in the egg yolk followed by the egg whites until well blended.

Pour the mixture into the prepared pan and put it on a deep-sided baking sheet. Quarter-fill the baking sheet with boiling water, then very carefully lift the sheet with the pan and water in it and place in the oven. Bake for 15 minutes, lightly moisten the extra circle of baking paper and cover the top of the risen cake. Reduce the oven setting to 350°F and cook for a further 20 minutes. Then turn off the oven and leave the cake in the cooling oven for another 20 minutes.

Remove and turn out on to a serving plate, or transfer to an airtight container or simply cut into slices and wrap them up for your picnic. This cake serves well with fresh raspberries (my son's favorite), or any wild sweet berries, mixed with crème fraîche.

homemade lemonade

This is one of those things I always imagine young children selling on the side of their street somewhere in the Midwest. If your son or daughter has aspirations to set up a stall, this is a great thing to start with. For best results you need to make a sugar syrup; alternatively, you can buy sugar syrup in bottles from specialist delicatessens or big supermarkets – it's usually French in origin.

Put the sugar in a saucepan and add 1⅓ pints (3 cups) water. Gently bring to a boil and remove from the heat. Add the ice cubes and stir until they have melted. Pour in the strained lemon juice and allow to cool to room temperature.

Place a funnel in the top of a 1¾ pint bottle and slowly pour in the lemonade. Put the lid on and chill for at least 6 hours.

4 ounces (½ cup) granulated sugar

4 ice cubes

9 fluid ounces (1 cup) lemon juice (about 6 lemons), strained

Makes 1¾ pints

orange pressé

Make as for the Lemonade, using 18 fluid ounces (2 cups) water and adding the lime juice and the Grand Marnier if you want. Chill again for at least 6 hours.

2 ounces (¼ cup) granulated sugar

4 ice cubes

18 fluid ounces (2 cups) freshly squeezed orange juice (about 8 oranges), strained

juice of 1 lime

a shot of Grand Marnier (if you fancy it)

Makes 4 glasses

Although bread and cheese are often eaten at the end of a meal, they can also be a meal in themselves – freshly baked bread and great cheese made all the more delicious with homemade pickle. It is believed that one of the first sorts of cheese made was similar to today's cottage or ricotta cheese. In the Middle East, milk was carried inside bags made from sheep's stomachs and the natural rennet in these, coupled with the heat of the sun, caused the milk to curdle into curds and whey. From these beginnings came cheeses like haloumi, feta, and ricotta. Obviously, over the years, the art of cheese-making has been perfected all over Europe to make some of our most complex and sophisticated foodstuffs.

bread, cheese, and pickles

ciabatta

Place 1 pound (4 cups) of the flour in a large mixing bowl and make a well in the middle. In a separate bowl, mix the yeast with 3½ fluid ounces (⅓ cup) water, until you have a paste. Pour the yeast paste into the well of the flour in the other bowl. Then add 11½ fluid ounces (1⅓ cups) water and mix to a sticky dough. Now use your hands to turn and beat the mixture for 5 minutes, until it is very elastic. Cover the bowl with a damp dish towel and leave it to rest for 4 hours. During this time the dough will rise spectacularly.

After four hours, knock back the dough, adding the olive oil and salt. Gradually add the rest of the flour and knead until you have a soft sticky dough. Cover the dough once again with the dish towel and leave for another hour. During this time the dough will rise again to double its size.

When it is risen, using a sharp knife, cut the dough in half, taking care not to handle the dough too much. Carefully tip each half into a baking pan. Your uncooked loaves should be roughly 1 inch thick and rectangular in shape. Sprinkle flour over the loaves and leave once more to rest for a further hour.

Preheat the oven to 425°F and bake the loaves for 35 minutes. Once cooked, place on a wire rack to cool.

1½ pounds (6 cups) unbleached white bread flour, plus more for dusting

1 ounce fresh yeast

5 fluid ounces (⅔ cup) extra-virgin olive oil

½ ounce (1 tablespoon) salt

Makes 2 loaves

You can tell when your ciabatta is cooked by tapping the base of the loaf, it should sound hollow.

For Olive Ciabatta, dust 7 ounces (2 cups) green olives with flour and fold into the dough before the second rising.

gingerbread

Preheat the oven to 350°F and grease a 2 pound loaf pan, then line the base with baking paper. In a large mixing bowl, sift the flour, ginger, cinnamon, baking powder, sodium bicarbonate, and salt. Mix together.

In a small saucepan over a low heat, melt the butter with the sugar, treacle, and syrup. Pull off the heat and leave to cool slightly. In a separate bowl, whisk the egg and milk together, then mix this into the flour. Finally add the syrup mixture and blend all the ingredients together well.

Pour the gingerbread batter into the prepared bread pan and bake in the oven for 50-70 minutes until a skewer inserted into the center comes out dry. Remove from the oven and allow to cool a little before turning out.

1 pound (4 cups) all-purpose flour

1 tablespoon ground ginger

1 teaspoon ground cinnamon

1 tablespoon baking powder

1 teaspoon sodium bicarbonate

a pinch of salt

4 ounces (1 stick) butter, plus more for greasing

1 ounce (2 tablespoons) light muscovado sugar

8 tablespoons treacle

8 tablespoons golden syrup

1 egg

5 fluid ounces (⅔ cup) milk

focaccia

In a large mixing bowl, mix the yeast with 5 fluid ounces (⅔ cup) cold water to form a paste. Add another 5 fluid ounces (⅔ cup) of water with 3 tablespoons of olive oil and mix together. Now add half of the flour and the salt, and blend well with the liquid. Gradually start to work in enough of the rest of the flour to form a soft, but not sticky, dough.

Tip the dough out on a lightly floured work surface and knead for at least 10 minutes until the dough is very smooth. Wash and dry the mixing bowl and grease it with olive oil. Place the dough back into the mixing bowl and move it around until it is lightly covered with oil. Cover the mixing bowl with a damp dish towel and leave it to rise for 2 hours.

Grease a 10 x 14 inch baking or roasting pan. When the dough is risen, knock it back and place it on a lightly floured work surface. Roll and shape the dough into a rectangular shape to fit the prepared pan. Place the dough in the pan and press the dough gently into all the corners. Cover the pan with a damp dish towel and leave to rise for another hour.

After this hour, using your fingers, make firm indentations about ½ inch deep all over the dough. Again, cover with a damp dish towel and leave to rise for 1-1½ hours, the dough should then have doubled in size.

Preheat the oven to 425°F. Once the dough has risen, drizzle olive oil over the surface, filling up the indentations, and sprinkle with the coarse sea salt. Put the baking pan in the oven and, using a water spray, spray the dough. Allow the focaccia dough to bake for 5 minutes and then spray it again with water. Bake for a further 25 minutes, until the bread is golden brown. Try to serve while still warm.

½ ounce fresh yeast

7 tablespoons extra-virgin olive oil, plus more for greasing

14 ounces (4½ cups) unbleached white bread flour, plus more for dusting

2 teaspoons salt

2 teaspoons coarse sea salt, for dusting

Makes 1 large loaf

soda bread

Preheat the oven to 425°F. In a mixing bowl, combine the flours, salt, and sodium bicarbonate. Using your fingers, rub the butter into the flour. As you do this, raise your hands and let the flour fall back into the bowl, this will help get air into the dough. Keep doing this until your mixture has a fine crumble consistency. Now start to stir in the buttermilk, adding enough to make a firm rough-looking dough. Flour a work surface and turn the dough out.

Knead the dough until smooth. Once smooth, shape it into a flat disc and place it on a baking sheet, dust with flour and score a deep cross over the surface of the disc. Bake in the oven for 40 minutes, until the loaf has a good brown crust. Allow to cool on a wire rack.

12 ounces (3 cups) stoneground wholewheat flour, plus more for dusting

4 ounces (1 cup) unbleached flour

1 teaspoon salt

1 teaspoon sodium bicarbonate

1 ounce (2 tablespoons) butter

12 fluid ounces (1⅓ cups) buttermilk

Makes 1 loaf

You can, of course, use a variety of different fruits in the muffins, like currants and raisins, cherries, apricots, dried and fresh, depending on what is in season.

blackberry muffins

5 ounces (1¼ cups) unbleached flour

5 ounces (1¼ cups) stoneground wholewheat bread flour

3 teaspoons baking powder

3 ounces (½ cup) superfine sugar

a pinch of salt

1 egg

10 fl. oz. (1¼ cups) milk

2 teaspoons lemon juice

2 ounces (½ stick) butter, melted

5 oz. (¾ cup) blackberries

oil, for greasing

Makes 12

Preheat the oven to 400°F and grease a 12-hole muffin pan. Sift both the flours and the baking powder into a large mixing bowl. Mix and add the sugar and pinch of salt. In a separate bowl, mix together the milk, egg, lemon juice, and melted butter. Pour this into the flour mix and gently mix together to a rough consistency. Add the blackberries and fold in gently.

Spoon the mixture into the muffin pan indentations and bake in the oven for 25 minutes, until risen and golden brown (don't worry if the tops of the muffins have cracks in them, they're supposed to). Allow your muffins to cool a little before turning them out on a wire rack.

herb rolls

butter, for greasing

1 pound (4 cups) unbleached white self raising flour, plus more for dusting

1 teaspoon salt

ground black pepper

2 tablespoons very finely chopped fresh herbs (oregano, marjoram, thyme, parsley, basil)

8 ounces (1 cup) cottage cheese

1 medium egg

8 fluid ounces (1 cup) milk, plus more for brushing

Makes 8–10

Preheat the oven to 350F° and grease and flour a baking sheet. Sift the flour, salt, and 4 twists of pepper into a large mixing bowl. Mix the herbs with the cottage cheese and egg, and gently stir this mixture into the flour. Add the milk a little, at a time, until you have a soft but not sticky dough.

Lightly flour a work surface, turn the dough out onto it and knead until smooth. Separate the dough into 8 equal balls, and place them on the baking sheet. Brush with a little milk and bake for 25 minutes until golden brown. Allow to cool on a wire rack.

date, apple, & walnut loaf

Preheat the oven to 350F° and prepare a 1 pound loaf pan by greasing the sides and lining the base with baking paper.

In a mixing bowl, cream the butter and sugar well. In a separate bowl, whisk the eggs, then add them to the creamed butter. Stir in the flour, walnuts, dates and apple to form a stiff dough, then add the milk. Empty the mixture into the loaf pan and level the surface.

Cook in the oven for 1-1¼ hours, until a skewer inserted into the center comes out dry. Remove and allow to cool a little before turning out. Pull away the baking paper and leave to cool fully on a wire rack.

olive oil, for greasing

4 oz. (1 stick) unsalted butter

4 ounces (½ cup) light muscovado sugar

2 eggs

4 oz. (1 cup) self-rising flour

4 ounces (1 cup) stone-ground wholewheat flour

4 oz. (1 cup) walnuts, chopped

4 ounces (⅔ cup) pitted dates, chopped

4 ounces peeled, cored, and shredded apple (preferably Granny Smith)

2 tablespoons milk

Makes 1 smallish loaf

The date, apple, and walnut loaf is wonderful served with a good mature Cheddar.

The thumbprint in the middle of each bap makes them cook flat rather than domed.

baps

1½ pounds (6 cups) unbleached white bread flour, plus more for dusting

1 tablespoon sea salt

½ ounce fresh yeast

1 teaspoon sugar

7½ fluid ounces (¾ cup) milk, plus more for glazing

7½ fluid ounces (¾ cup) lukewarm water

2 ounces (4 tablespoons) lard, cut into small chunks

vegetable oil, for greasing

Put the flour and salt in a large bowl. In another bowl, mix the yeast with the sugar and a tablespoon each of the lukewarm water and milk. Mix to a smooth paste. Add the lard and, using your fingers, blend it into the flour until it becomes a fine crumble. Make a well in the middle and pour in the yeast paste, now pour in the rest of the milk and water and mix together to form a very soft, but not sticky, dough. Turn this out on a lightly floured work surface and knead it for 10 minutes until very smooth.

Wash the mixing bowl, dry it and lightly grease with vegetable oil. Put the dough back in the mixing bowl and cover the bowl with a damp dish towel, leave the dough to rise for 1–1½ hours, or until it has doubled in size.

Grease 2 baking sheets and put them to one side. Knock the dough back and once again turn it out on a lightly floured work surface. Knead it a little and then divide it into 12 equal pieces. Put a little flour on your fingers and mold and roll each piece of dough into an oval shape about ½ inch thick and 3 inches in length. Once each bap is shaped, place them on one of the 2 baking sheets, leaving as much space as you can between them. Lightly brush them with milk and sift with flour. Now leave to rise for about 30 minutes, again to double their size, but no more!

Preheat the oven to 425°F. Sift a heavier layer of flour over the risen baps and, using your thumb, make a ¼ inch deep print in the center of each. Bake for 15 minutes until golden. Remove and place on a wire rack to cool a little.

cheese

Cheese is one of those foods people either love or hate. Once you've entered this fascinating world, it is quite addictive, not just as a food, but in wanting to know how it's made, why, and how milk can end up as Brie, Roquefort, or Parmesan when the original ingredients are so similar.

Although I've always loved cheese, I only really started to study its production about 2 years ago, and was amazed how storage and temperature and different bacteria can affect this commodity as much as it does. The practice of cheese-making is comparable to the making of fine wine. The environment in which you make your cheese also affects the outcome of your cheese. From the caves of Roquefort and Cheddar Gorge to my larder at work, it all tastes so different. There are many wonderful cheeses that are harder to find in supermarkets, though with a little research and the help of a good cheese book and supplier you can find incredibly diverse cheeses, some possibly being made on your doorstep.

Here is a simple method for making your own cheese. Do ensure while maturing the cheese that the temperature doesn't rise above 36°F.
Pour 2 pints of milk into a saucepan, add the finely shredded rind of 1 lemon and slowly warm the milk to blood temperature, then keep the milk at this constant temperature for 1 hour. This will separate the curds from the whey, forming lumps on the surface of the milk. Allow to cool.
   Once cooled, pour the mixture through a strainer. Discard the whey and add the curd to a bowl. Season it well with salt. Pour the salted curds on to a piece of cheesecloth, gather the cheesecloth around the whey and squeeze it into a tight ball, allowing any excess moisture to drain out of the cheesecloth. Tie the bag up and hang it over a bowl in the refridgerator for 2 days.
   After 2 days you can eat the cheese; which will be similar to ricotta.

pickles

My first major introduction to the preserving of vegetables and fruits was while I was working one summer as chef on an estate in Tuscany. To keep up with the volume of fruit and vegetables, there was a frantic hotbed of activity, in which we would jar, bottle, pickle and sun-dry up to two-thirds of what was coming into the larder every day. Crates and jars would be scrubbed, boiled, and filled with anything from fig chutney to oil-preserved eggplant. In the following months, diving into the homemade chutneys was a wonderfully nostalgic reminder of the summer.

redcurrant jelly

Put the redcurrants, including stalks if they are still on, into a large saucepan. Add 1 pint of water and the spices. Bring to a boil and simmer until the redcurrants are mushed, pushing them a spoon until you have a purée, about 20 minutes.

Strain into a saucepan through a fine strainer or a piece of cheesecloth, pushing with the back of a spoon. Add the vinegar and sugar, bring to a boil and boil for about 15 minutes, or until syrupy.

Pour the syrup into sterilized jars and cover while still hot to create a vacuum in the jars. Store in a cool dry place.

2 pounds redcurrants
3 cloves
1 cinnamon stick
¼ pint (⅔ cup) malt vinegar
2 pounds (4 cups) granulated sugar

Makes about 4½ pounds

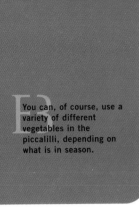

You can, of course, use a variety of different vegetables in the piccalilli, depending on what is in season.

traditional piccalilli

Just the thought makes me sweat under the eyes. This is one of my favorite accompaniments for cold meats, pies, and hard cheeses. It is best made in reasonably large quantities as, once made, it can be kept in the refridgerator for up to a month.

½ small cauliflower, roughly chopped

2 medium carrots

5 baby sweetcorns, sliced

1 zucchini, cubed

2 celery stalks, sliced

2 small green tomatoes, roughly chopped

1 large cucumber, roughly sliced

10 small shallots, halved lengthwise

9 ounces (1¼ cups) cooking salt

2½ pints (5¼ cups) plus 4 tablespoons clear malt vinegar

8 ounces (1 cup) granulated sugar

1 tablespoon ground turmeric

1 tablespoon mustard powder

½ teaspoon ground ginger

4 garlic cloves, finely cubed

2 small chiles, seeded and finely chopped

2 tablespoons cornstarch

Makes about 5 pints

In a large bowl, mix together the cauliflower, carrots, sweetcorn, zucchini, celery, tomatoes, cucumber, and shallots with the salt. Leave to sit overnight.

The following day, rinse all the vegetables well and drain. In a large saucepan, mix the 2½ pints vinegar with the sugar, turmeric, mustard, ginger, garlic, and chile, and bring to a boil. Add all the vegetables and allow to simmer. Cover the simmering vegetables and allow to cook until just starting to soften, about 5 minutes. Add the cornstarch and stir, then add the extra 4 tablespoons of vinegar and continue stirring until your mixture starts to bubble and thicken. Spoon the hot Piccalilli into sterilized jars and seal immediately.

mint & apple jelly

This delicious relish goes well with lamb, pork, or game.

Roughly chop the apples, but do not peel or core. Remove the mint leaves from the stalks, discard the stalks and finely chop the leaves. Add the chopped apples, three-quarters of the mint, the lemon juice, and mineral water to a large saucepan. Bring the mixture to a boil, then reduce to a simmer. Cover and continue simmering until the apple is very soft, about 40 minutes.

Slowly strain the mixture through a large fine dish towel, cloth or piece of cheesecloth into a heatproof bowl. Do not squeeze or press the mixture through the cloth as this will make your jelly cloudy rather than brilliantly clear. Once all the mixture is strained, discard any remaining pulp.

Now measure the apple liquid and, for every 9 fluid ounces (1 cup) of liquid, add 5½ ounces (¾ cup) of sugar. Heat in a large, deep saucepan until the sugar is dissolved. Then boil, without covering or stirring, for 30 minutes. Remove from the heat and allow to stand for 5 minutes.

Stir in the remaining mint. Pour the jelly into sterilized jars and seal. This will keep in the refrigerator for up to 2 months.

7 medium apples

a bunch of fresh mint

5 tablespoons lemon juice

2¾ pints (6¼ cups) mineral water

about 1½ pound (3 cups) granulated sugar

Makes about 1¼ pints

fig & madeira chutney

Cut the fresh figs into eighths and combine with all the other ingredients in a large saucepan. Stir over a moderate heat, making sure your mixture does not come to a boil. Once all the sugar is dissolved, simmer uncovered for about 2½–3 hours, stirring occasionally until the mixture starts to thicken.

Spoon the hot chutney into sterilized jars and seal immediately. This chutney will store in a cool dark place for up to 6 months; refrigerate once opened.

16 large ripe fresh figs

6 fluid ounces (¾ cup) Madeira

2 large onions, finely chopped

6 ounces (1 cup) raisins, chopped

2 teaspoons shredded fresh ginger

2 small fresh red chiles, seeded and finely chopped

1 pound (2 cups) granulated sugar

1¼ pints (3 cups) malt vinegar

2 teaspoons grainy mustard

Makes about 2¼ pounds

lime pickle with lemon grass

Quarter the limes, put them in a large mixing bowl and mix with the salt, then leave to sit overnight.

    The following day, rinse the limes in cold water and drain. Remove the cilantro leaves whole from the stems and chop the stems very finely, discarding any woody bits.

    Heat the olive oil in a large saucepan and add the chiles, ginger, garlic, lemon grass, mustard, cardamom, and cilantro stalks. Stir for a couple of minutes, then add the limes and vinegar and bring to a boil. Allow to simmer, uncovered, for 10-15 minutes. Once cooled, mix in the cilantro leaves.

    Spoon the pickle into sterilized jars. This will keep in the fridge for up to one month.

10 medium limes

2 teaspoons rock salt

a bunch of fresh cilantro

¼ pint (1 cup) olive oil

4 small green chiles, seeded and chopped

1 teaspoon freshly shredded ginger

6 garlic cloves, finely chopped

1 lemon grass stalk, finely chopped

1 teaspoon grainy mustard

2 teaspoons cardamom seeds

18 fluid ounces (2 cups) clear malt vinegar

Makes about 2¼ pints

pear & apple chutney

Wash and dry the pears and apples well, then cut them into quarters and discard the cores, then cut them again into small rough cubes.

    In a large saucepan, mix the fruit with all the other ingredients and stir over a low heat until all the sugar has dissolved. Continue to simmer, stirring occasionally, for about 1½ hours; by then your mixture should have thickened.

    Spoon the hot chutney into sterilized jars, seal and store in a cool dark place. This chutney should keep for up to 6 months in this way; once opened, however, you must refrigerate.

6 medium pears

3 medium apples

1 large onion, finely chopped

10 cherry tomatoes, quartered

14 ounces (1¾ cups) brown sugar

5 ounces (1 cup) golden raisins

2¾ ounces dried apricots, chopped

18 fluid ounces (2 cups) cider vinegar

9 fluid ounces (1 cup) still cider (if not available, use dry white wine)

1 tablespoon grainy mustard

2 garlic cloves, finely chopped

½ teaspoon ground cinnamon

½ teaspoon ground cardamom

1 teaspoon dried sage

1 teaspoon dried oregano

Makes about 1¼ pints

peach & champagne chutney

Blanch the peaches in boiling water for 10 seconds, then remove the skins and stones, and chop roughly.

Make a bouquet garni: place the ingredients together in a small piece of cheesecloth and tie up securely.

Place this in a saucepan with all the other ingredients and stir over a moderate heat, without boiling, allowing it to simmer for 1½ hours, stirring occasionally. Once the mixture has thickened, remove the bouquet garni.

Spoon the chutney into sterilized jars and seal immediately. This will keep for up to 6 months in a cool dark place; refrigerate once opened.

7 peaches

2 Spanish onions, finely chopped

14 ounces (1¾ cups) brown sugar

5 ounces (1 cup) golden raisins

3 tablespoons shredded fresh ginger

2 garlic cloves, finely chopped

6 tablespoons fresh lime juice

14 fluid ounces (1½ cups) Champagne vinegar

1 glass of Champagne or sparkling wine

for the bouquet garni

2 dried red chiles

2 cloves

1 cinnamon stick

Makes about 1¾ pints

Sauces often accompany dishes of all kinds – meat, poultry, game, fish, and even vegetable dishes – and are traditionally served hot, poured over the food. It is vital when making sauces to start with a good broth to ensure a smooth and rich flavor. As always, an element of concentration is required to get the best results. Even something as simple as broiled chops or poached fish, when served with a great sauce, can be elevated to something really different. For example, broiled sausages, carrots, and mash can be made that bit more exciting with a generous serving of cider and mustard sauce. The following recipes are what I believe to be the basic essential sauces, but please feel free to innovate.

sauces and dressings

One thing you must ensure when adding the infusion is that you add just the liquid and not any of the spices and herbs.

hollandaise

Hollandaise can be used in many different ways, from being spooned over poached eggs and ham and broiled to make Eggs Benedict (page 22), to being folded into chilled fish sauces, being used as a glaze, or simply dressing just about any fish.

First make the infusion: place all the infusion ingredients into a saucepan, bring to a boil and reduce by half. Pull from the heat and allow to cool.

In a bain-marie (or heatproof bowl set over a saucepan half-filled with gently simmering water), clarify the butter by gently melting it until it separates, with the fat rising to the surface and the whey at the bottom. Remove the bowl from the heat, carefully ladle the clear butter into a heatproof container and place to one side. Discard the whey, wash the heatproof bowl and dry thoroughly.

Now place the egg yolks in the mixing bowl with 2 tablespoons of the strained infusion and, ensuring the water in the saucepan under the bowl is on moderate heat, whisk continuously until the yolks start to become firm. Remove the bowl from the heat and place on a flat surface. Wrap a dish towel around the bowl, to stop it slipping, whilst mixing. Start to whisk the egg yolks vigorously and, while whisking, slowly start to add the clarified butter. Keep slowly pouring in the butter until it is all blended. Continue whisking, while adding one more dessertspoon of the infusion, and whisk until fully blended. Finally add a pinch each of salt and cayenne pepper.

6 ounces (1½ sticks) butter

4 egg yolks

a pinch of salt

a pinch of cayenne pepper

for the infusion

5 tablespoons white wine vinegar

5 tablespoons white wine

5 black peppercorns

1 garlic clove

2–3 parsley stalks

juice of 1 lemon

béarnaise sauce

The ingredients for this are much the same as for Hollandaise Sauce, but with the addition of a bunch of fresh tarragon. Prepare the tarragon by separating the leaves from the stalks. Finely chop the leaves and place to one side; finely chop the stalks and add them to the infusion. Otherwise make exactly like the infusion for Hollandaise Sauce. Continue as for making Hollandaise and mix in the finely chopped tarragon leaves with the salt and cayenne. The anise-flavored essential oils in tarragon help break down proteins and fats, which is why it is generally served with red meats. It is also delicious.

anglo-french
broths & sauces

Although this style of sauce-making could keep you busy for years in the quest for perfection, and you could easily write many books on the subject, I have selected two simple bases for the creation of a small range of sauces. However, you could easily branch out from here on your own creative whim. The essence of any good sauce made in this style is starting off with a very good fresh broth. Only fresh broth will do and, fortunately, it can now be bought in cartons at your local supermarket.

If using veal or fish broth, when you buy either of these off the shelf, they are generally very pale in color and it is common practice, if a darker sauce color is required, to add tomato purée. Personally I avoid doing this, as you end up with a bitter, unpleasant flavor. It is far better to use fresh tomatoes, reduced down, as they taste far sweeter and color your sauce just as well.

This method of sauce-making always sets me in medieval mode: gizzards for game broths and the traditions of thickening chicken sauces with blood, for example, are not quite so commonplace any more. Modern sauce-making tends to avoid using roux and large quantities of cream, for obvious health reasons. But I will let you in on a taster of the tradition.

for dark sauces
(like red wine, port, & madeira sauces)

These make perfect accompaniments for red meat, but with fish broth base, they can be served with fish such as halibut, cod, or turbot.

Gently melt the butter with the olive oil in a large heavy saucepan. Increase the heat and add the carrots, shallots, celery, garlic, and herb stalks. Cook over a moderate heat until well softened. Now add the tomatoes and cook for 5–10 minutes until softened.

Stir in the sugar and then pour over the red wine. Reduce by half over a moderate heat, then add the broth and reduce again by two-thirds. Gently pass the mixture through a strainer or chinois into another saucepan and season. Your sauce is now ready to serve. You can keep the sauce in the fridge for up to 2 days.

variations
To make light sauces, like Calvados or Cider & Mustard Sauce, make as dark sauces but omit the tomatoes.

calvados sauce
Add a cored chopped cooking apple instead chopped tomato, and a wine glass of Calvados instead of the wine, gently reducing by half.

cider & mustard
Substitute cider for wine and, at the last moment after you have strained your sauce, add a teaspoon of grainy mustard and 2 tablespoons of heavy cream. Do not over-boil sauce once you have added your cream or it will separate.

For roast meats the same sauce-making principal can be applied. Once the meat has been cooked and removed to rest, pour away the fat and use the roasting pan instead of a saucepan, in this way you harness the flavors of the just-roasted meat with your sauce. This method is known as deglazing.

If making a sauce with aromatic flavorings, for example: wild mushroom or chestnut and sage, chop your preferred vegetables and gently sauté in the saucepan you'll be straining your sauce into. One of my favorite sauces made in this way is Madeira sauce.

Different sauces can be created by using a different alcohol instead of the wine, such as port for lamb, Madeira for beef; if using spirits use half the amount to that of wine. Always pull your pan off the heat to add fortified wines or spirits, as the alcohol has a tendency to flame.

---

2 ounces (½ stick) butter

3 tablespoons olive oil

2 large carrots, roughly chopped

4 largish shallots, finely chopped

2 celery stalks, chopped

4 garlic cloves, finely chopped

a few fresh herb stalks (rosemary for lamb, thyme for beef, sage for pork, a combination of thyme and chopped soft fruits for duck and game)

4 tomatoes, quartered

1 teaspoon sugar

½ bottle of red wine

1 pint (2½ cups) broth (veal broth for meat dishes; fish broth for fish, etc.)

roquefort sauce

Makes about 12 fluid ounces (1½ cups)

This French Alpine classic is one of my favorites, served with broiled steak. Yet again, it is the bacteria within the Roquefort's blue veining that aids digestion (don't panic, penicillin is a bacteria, as is yeast.) The same principle of sauce-making as opposite applies, sautéing vegetables in oil and butter, adding herb stalks, with half a bottle of white wine and reducing by half, then 1 pint (2½ cups) of veal broth, reducing by two-thirds, passing it through a strainer into a second saucepan and skimming off any excess oil on the surface of the sauce. Break 2 ounces (⅓ cup) of Roquefort cheese into small pieces, bring the skimmed sauce up to a simmer and whisk in the Roquefort with 2 tablespoons heavy cream. Season and serve. As well as being great with beef and veal, it is wonderful as a hot salad dressing.

caramelized shallots

These make a wonderful accompaniment to roast meats and game, served in the sauce.

Preheat the oven to 325°F and oil an oven sheet. Slice the unpeeled shallots (3 per person) lengthwise, sprinkle them with a pinch each of sugar and salt, place on the prepared sheet and cook in the oven for 20–30 minutes until well colored and softened. Peel the crisp skin away from the shallots and place the shallots in the pan into which you are straining your red wine sauce. Season with chopped fresh thyme.

traditional roman sauces

The following four simple Italian sauces date back to the Ancient Romans, who were all for combining the medicinal benefits of herbs with food.

salsa verde

This is one of my favorite sauces to accompany broiled — and most — meats, and is probably best described as the Italian version of mint sauce. As with many of the herbs used in cooking, the combination of vinegar and mint aids digestion.

Finely chop together the garlic, anchovy, and capers. Place in a large bowl and mix together to form a paste. Add the remaining ingredients, except the oil. Stir together and, as you are stirring, slowly add the olive oil. Adjust the seasoning, chill and serve.

1 garlic clove, salted and finely chopped

5 anchovy fillets, chopped

1 teaspoon capers

a bunch of fresh mint, finely chopped

a bunch of flat-leaf parsley, finely chopped

1 teaspoon Dijon mustard

1 tablespoon red wine vinegar

salt and pepper

6 tablespoons olive oil

Serves 4–6

variation

If serving with beef, you could add 1–2 tablespoon(s) of horseradish sauce.

salsa dragoncella

This simple-to-prepare salsa is wonderful with chicken, boiled meats like ham, and other cold meats.

Using a cheese shredder, gently shred the hard-cooked eggs into a mixing bowl. Stir in the tarragon, capers, mustard, and garlic. Now add the olive oil and red wine vinegar with salt and pepper to taste, and mix well. Place to one side or chill in refrigerator.

3 hard-cooked eggs, shelled

a bunch of fresh tarragon, finely chopped

1 teaspoon capers, drained and finely chopped

1 tablespoon Dijon mustard

1 garlic clove, finely chopped

3 tablespoons olive oil

4 teaspoons red wine vinegar

salt and pepper

gremolata

Traditionally gremolata is a form of condiment, combining salt, lemon rind, and chopped parsley to season meats while they are being cooked, as with *osso buco*. In my opinion you can take a bit of a broader view with gremolata, using a herb and citrus fruit of your choice to season your meat and fish. For example, chopped oregano, lime rind, and salt sprinkled over sea bass is delicious; as is chopped rosemary, lemon, and salt for lamb; chopped lime and orange rind, and salt for chicken and veal; or chopped sage, lemon, and shredded apple skin for pork dishes.

A variation on this theme, *salmoriglio* (see page 102), grinds salt and soft-leafed herbs together to a mush, then mixes this with olive oil to drizzle over cooked meats and fish.

salsa rossa

This is a great sauce for barbecues and one of my favorite fillings to spoon into jacket potatoes.

Preheat the oven to 350°F. Lightly toss the red peppers and the chile in olive oil and roast in the oven, turning them every 5–10 minutes, until all sides are well cooked and the skin blackened, 20–25 minutes in total. Put the peppers and chile in a bowl and immediately cover the bowl with plastic wrap. Place to one side.

    Mix the anchovies, garlic, and basil in a bowl. Chop the tomato pulp into cubes and add to the mixing bowl. Place to one side.

    Carefully remove the stalk and seeds from each pepper and the chile. Remove any blackened skin. Chop the cleaned pepper into small cubes, finely chop the chile and mix into the bowl, together with the vinegar, salt and pepper, and a touch of olive oil. Mix well and serve in a large bowl, like a salad.

6 red bell peppers

1 red chile, finely chopped

olive oil

2 anchovy fillets, finely chopped

2 garlic cloves, finely chopped

a bunch of fresh basil, finely chopped

4 tomatoes, blanched, skinned and seeded

2 teaspoons red wine vinegar

salt and pepper

fish broth & sauces

I always feel that fish sauces should only be served with a completely boned piece of fish, while fish on the bone like sea bass, sole or sardines, is best served simply with either a salsa or lemon juice, as you need a clean space on your plate to remove the fish from the bone.

pernod sauce

This sauce goes wonderfully well with filleted fish.

Gently melt the butter with the olive oil in a saucepan. Add the garlic, vegetables, star anise, fennel seeds, and parsley stalks but not the leaves. Bung in the Pernod or Ouzo and reduce by half. Add the fish broth and gently reduce by two-thirds. Strain into another saucepan and add the cream, the finely chopped parsley leaves, and salt and pepper to taste. Bring back to a boil for 1 minute and serve.

variations

oriental fish sauce

Substitute sake for the Pernod or Ouzo, and soy sauce for the cream, but only 2 tablespoons and don't add salt.

italian fish sauce

Substitute white wine for the Pernod or Ouzo, 2 tablespoons of lemon juice for the heavy cream, and 2 tablespoons of freshly chopped and seeded tomatoes, and fresh basil instead of, or as well as, the parsley.

2 ounces (½ stick) butter

2 tablespoons olive oil

4 garlic cloves, finely chopped

3 shallots, finely chopped

1 carrot, finely chopped

2 celery stalks, finely chopped

1 fennel bulb, finely chopped

4 star anise

1 tablespoon fennel seeds (if available)

a bunch of parsley, finely chopped but stalks retained

a wine glass of Pernod or Ouzo (not sambuca, which might make some of your guests mad)

1 pint (2½ cups) fish broth

4 tablespoons heavy cream

salt and pepper

salsa di panicalli

I had to add this unusual fish sauce firstly because it does accompany broiled fish beautifully and also to dedicate it to a most interesting man who gave me his secret recipe, Oraldo Panicalli. So not to contradict myself, this is more of a salsa than a sauce and will not inhibit but enhance the eating of fish on the bone.

Combine all the ingredients in a large mixing bowl. Whisk well and serve.

3 rosemary sprigs, stripped from the stalks (but reserve these as they are useful as skewers)

a bunch of chives, finely chopped

1 garlic clove, crushed

2 tablespoons balsamic vinegar

2 tablespoons Worcestershire Sauce

juice of 1 lemon

4 tablespoons olive oil

salt and pepper

2 drops of Tabasco sauce

1 teaspoon Dijon mustard

dressings

Dressings are easiest made with a blender; if one isn't available, pre-chop your ingredients and then blend using a whisk and bowl — and lots of elbow grease. The advantage of a blender is that it chops and whisks all at once, to emulsify your ingredients. However, all these recipes were around long before the invention of electrical kitchen devices.

traditional salad dressing

This dressing is a recipe I learnt from Stephan, a German chef I worked for while on a yacht in France. He used to say, 'Edward you will always remember me, a hard taskmaster.' I don't really want to remember him, but his recipes and cooking were second to none. This is our house dressing at Randall & Aubin and has been guarded for the past 6 years. Due to a good publishing deal, though, I am now prepared to release it!

Put the onion, anchovy, and garlic in a blender or food processor and blitz for 30 seconds.

With the blender still running, add the egg yolk and slowly start to add half the olive oil (the stream looking like the 'tail of a mouse'). Now add half the warm water, still continuing to blend, and then slowly add the remaining oil followed by the remaining water. Add the vinegar and turn off the blender.

Stir in the lemon juice, parsley, mustard, and salt and pepper to taste. This will keep for a week in the fridge.

¼ Spanish onion

1 anchovy fillet

1 garlic clove

1 egg yolk

¼ pint (⅔ cup) olive oil

3 tablespoons lukewarm water

2 tablespoons white wine vinegar

juice of ½ lemon

a small bunch (¼ ounce) of parsley, finely chopped

1 tablespoon grainy mustard

salt and pepper

Serves 6
(makes ½–¾ pint)

caesar dressing

Caesar salad is always one of those big sellers and, no matter what restaurant menu I write, caesar salad always seems to end up on it, by popular demand. Mind you there is caesar salad and there is caesar salad, and I've had a few sad caesars in my time.

A good caesar dressing should be tangy and similar in texture to mayonnaise. A top food critic once said that a restaurant can be judged by their caesar salad. Every year we sell thousands of caesar salads made to the following recipe, to the point of addiction for some of our regular customers. The most bizarre request came from a customer who regularly orders a caesar salad with no anchovy — a quick look at the recipe below and you will realize why this is such an odd request.

To make the dressing: put the garlic, anchovy fillets, and lemon juice in a blender or food processor and blitz. After one minute, with the machine still running, add the egg yolks, then slowly start to add the olive oil, ensuring that the oil emulsifies with the egg yolks. When two-thirds of the oil is incorporated, pour in 3 tablespoons of warm water, with the blender still running, then add the Worcestershire sauce, Tabasco, and tomato ketchup. Then slowly add the remaining oil and turn off the blender.

Pour the Caesar dressing into a large bowl. Add the chopped parsley and Parmesan cheese with a good twist of black pepper. Salt is not necessary.

Caesar salad is traditionally served with croutons. To make them, pan-fry the bread cubes in olive oil, as you would fried bread. Remove from the pan and drain on paper towels.

Discarding the outer leaves, shred the lettuce and mix well in the bowl with the dressing and the croutons. (You'll probably need to use two mixing bowls, or use the same bowl mixing bowl twice if you are serving individual salads.) Serve sprinkled with more Parmesan.

3 Romaine lettuces

for the dressing:
2 garlic cloves
1¼ ounces of anchovy fillets
juice of 1 lemon
2 egg yolks
11 fluid ounces (1⅓ cups) olive oil
3 tablespoons warm water
1 tablespoon Worcestershire sauce
4 drops of Tabasco sauce
1 tablespoon tomato ketchup
a bunch (1½ ounces) of parsley
5 ounces (2¼ cups) Parmesan cheese, shredded, plus more to serve
pepper

for the croutons
4–5 thick slices of white bread, cut into small cubes
olive oil, for frying

Serves 6

basil dressing

Mozzarella and tomato salad springs to mind here, but this dressing goes well with just about any salad, especially those with cheese. It is also a great dressing for grilled vegetables, and can be kept in the refridgerator for a couple of weeks.

Heat about 6 tablespoons of the olive oil in a skillet and lightly fry the pine nuts over a moderate heat. As the pine nuts start to brown, remove them from the heat and allow to cool in the oil.

In a blender, blitz the garlic with the lemon juice, then add the chopped basil. Turn off the blender, add the pine nuts and their oil, and pulse the blender for 3–4 seconds (this helps keep the sauce a little bit crunchy). Now add the remaining olive oil and the shredded Parmesan with salt and pepper to taste and again pulse for 3–4 seconds.

Pour into a clean bottle or jar. This will keep for up to a week in the refrigerator.

12 fluid ounces (1½ cups) olive oil

a handful of pine nuts

1 garlic clove

juice of 2 lemons

a bunch of basil, finely chopped

7 ounces (3 cups) Parmesan cheese, shredded

salt and pepper

french dressing

The easiest way to make this simple dressing is with an old jam jar – make sure it's one with a re-sealable lid. For me, this is the perfect dressing for avocado, tomato, and onion salads, or for dressing green beans or spring vegetables.

Put all the ingredients in the jar (see above), with salt and pepper to taste. Place the lid on jar and shake vigorously for 30 seconds. Voilà, French Dressing.

1 egg yolk

2 tablespoons white wine vinegar

8 tablespoons olive oil

1 teaspoon Dijon mustard

salt and pepper

Makes ¼ pint

I always think it's funny how people grudge spending more than a couple of dollars on olive oil and balsamic vinegar and yet happily pay fifteen for a bottle of wine that's gone in one meal.

balsamic dressing

The simple fact is that the more money you throw at this dressing the better it will taste. Two components to a good balsamic dressing are excellent-quality balsamic vinegar and the best extra-virgin olive oil available, though how can you be extra-virgin? Answers on a postcard...

An alternative to blowing your week's budget on salad dressing – and one that I use to great effect – is using standard balsamic vinegar and reducing it gently by one-third. This will thicken it and enrich the flavor. Once it has cooled, mix three parts oil to one part vinegar, a squeeze of lemon juice and a twist of black pepper, then give it a good whisk.

This dressing goes beautifully with arugula and most green salads, as well as vegetable salads such as green bean and zucchini.

blue cheese dressing

This is one of my fondest favorites for chip-dipping and pouring over steaks and burgers. Is also a must for any barbecue buffet. Roquefort is often used (see page 243), but for this recipe I use Stilton, as it is slightly milder.

1 egg yolk
1 garlic clove
4 ounces (¾ cup) Stilton cheese
1 tablespoon warm water
9 fluid ounces (1 cup) olive oil
juice of 1 lemon
a bunch of tarragon, chopped

Makes about ¾ pint

Blitz the egg yolk and garlic in a blender or food processor, at the same time slowly crumbling in the cheese. When half the cheese is incorporated, pour in the tablespoon of warm water and allow the ingredients to blend. With the machine still running, slowly add the olive oil. When all the oil is incorporated, add the remaining cheese and lemon juice and blend for another 20 seconds. Turn off the blender and fold in the chopped tarragon. Chill until ready to use (this will keep for up to 2 days, covered, in the refrigerator.)

index